OPPORTUNITIES IN
JOURNALISM

John Tebbel

Vocational Guidance Manuals
A Division of Data Courier, Inc.
Louisville, Kentucky

Publisher–Loene Trubkin
Editor–Christine Maddox
Assistant Editor–Gary Barker
Photo Editor–Donna Lawrence
Production Manager–Carmen Chetti
Production Supervisor–Sylvia Ward
Production–Tammy Crumpton
Administrative Services–Cynthia Pierce

Manufactured in the
United States of America

Library of Congress Catalog Card Number 76–14060

ISBN Number   0-89022-226-6 (Hardcover)
                0-89022-227-4 (Paperbound)

Cover photograph by Charlie Westerman

ABOUT THE AUTHOR

John Tebbel began his newspaper career at fourteen, when he went to work for a newspaper in Shepherd, Michigan. He did correspondence work for state dailies and wire services throughout high school and college. In 1935, the first year after his graduation from Central Michigan University, he became city editor of the Mt. Pleasant, Michigan, *Times-News.* Later he attended the Graduate School of Journalism at Columbia University (M.S. 1937), and while still there, began working for *Newsweek* magazine as a junior staff writer. He was a reporter for the *Detroit Free Press,* Sunday feature writer and editor for the *Providence Journal,* managing editor of the *American Mercury,* and Sunday staff writer for the New York *Times* before he left the newspaper business to go into book publishing as associate editor of E. P. Dutton & Co.

At the end of 1946, he resigned to write books, and since then he has written nearly forty books of his own and as many in various kinds of collaboration. Mr. Tebbel has also written more than 300 articles for national magazines. For ten years he was a regular monthly contributor to the Communications Section of the *Saturday Review.*

After six years on the part-time faculty of the Graduate School of Journalism at Columbia, Mr. Tebbel began teaching full-time in the Department of Journalism at New York University in 1949. He became chairman of the department in 1954 and remained in that post until 1965, except for four years on leave to be director of the Graduate Institute of Book Publishing at N.Y.U. From 1965 until his retirement in 1976, he was Professor of Journalism at N.Y.U. (now Professor Emeritus).

Mr. Tebbel continues to pursue his parallel career of writing books and magazine articles and has written in many areas, including eleven books in the field of communications. The first volume of his four-volume *History of Book Publishing in the United States* (two have been published) was nominated for a Pulitzer Prize in 1972.

INTRODUCTION

Interest in journalism as a career is at an all-time high, and John Tebbel's book is an important contribution to journalism career education. Mr. Tebbel has worked with care and precision to select the most current data for inclusion in this volume.

It is fitting that "Newspapering as a Way of Life" should be the title of Chapter One, because newspapers are the way of life for John Tebbel. His distinguished career includes reporting, editing, publishing, and college journalism teaching. Certainly, to others of us in the business, newspapering is also a way of life. For young people who are considering making journalism their way of life, Mr. Tebbel outlines well what that life might be like. It is a realistic appraisal, which discusses both the good and bad points of a journalism career.

Any young person who wants to know more about the substance and scope of news work will be enlightened by the information on the following pages. John Tebbel's wise and timely advice should be taken to heart by all aspiring journalists.

Thomas E. Engleman
Executive Director
The Newspaper Fund

TABLE OF CONTENTS

The masculine pronoun and the term "newspaperman" are used in this book in their generic sense for reasons of clarity and succinctness. They are intended, of course, to refer to females as well as males.

CHAPTER 1

NEWSPAPERING AS A WAY OF LIFE

To call working for newspapers a way of life instead of simply a career goes to the heart of what journalism is all about. It implies not only a commitment, the kind that would be required for going into the other professions, but a willingness to become a particular kind of person, one who becomes a trained observer of human events rather than a direct participant in them.

Reporters have a front row seat for these events—fires, crimes, conventions, the appearance of celebrities, politics, whatever—and so it appears to those on the outside, the people who sit at home and read about it in the papers, that the newspaper reporter himself is involved. But in the ordinary course of events he is involved only as an observer, the person who reports what he sees, or who tries to determine what actually happened after an event takes place.

Newspapering is not all reporting what happens, by any means, as we'll see later on. Behind every man and woman who is out of the city room on assignment is a larger group of people—those who edit what is written, who decide what stories are to be covered, who process news that comes into the office from other cities and countries by wire, who take the pictures that go into the paper and edit them; not to mention the specialists who handle sports, theater, film, books, editorials, columns, and the other departments of a paper.

What do all these people have in common? First of all, they have a consuming curiosity about the world and everything that's in it. People who are not intensely interested in what goes on around them would be well advised to go into some other field. Another primary characteristic of newspaper people is something that used to be called "a nose for news," although this phrase isn't heard much any more. Whatever it's called, it is essential. There are several old jokes in the business about reporters who didn't have it. One concerns the new reporter (they were once called "cubs") who was sent out to cover the wedding of two people prominent in society and returned to tell his editor regretfully, "Sorry, boss, but there's no story. The bride didn't show up." A much more apocryphal story tells of the young reporter assigned to cover a natural disaster in a nearby town who telegraphed back to his city editor: "All is confusion. Can send nothing."

If you don't get the point of either of these ancient jokes, the chances are you'll never be a newspaper reporter. You must know news when you see it. It's a difficult thing to define, although many people have nevertheless tried to define it. Obviously, a three-alarm fire, a murder, a natural catastrophe like a flood or a tornado, or a political leader accused of a civil or criminal offense—all these unquestionably constitute news. But one of the common definitions, "News is anything that happens," isn't quite accurate, because sometimes news is something that *doesn't* happen, like the society girl who didn't show up for her wedding.

Another definition, "news is anything of interest," comes closer to the mark, if we define "interest" as involving the interests of large numbers of people. Thus, if Mr. and Mrs. Smith have a family quarrel, and Mr. Smith packs his bag and walks out, that is of no interest to anyone except the Smiths and their families, and possibly the neighbors. But if the quarreling couple happen to be celebrities, in show business or political life, a great many people are sure to be interested in the outcome and so it becomes news.

What happens to people in public life is news, and so is anything that affects the broad interests of people—happenings in business and finance, sports, the arts, religion, politics, sex, and so on. The relative importance of these happenings to each other depends on the news judgments of editors, and among experienced professionals, these judgments are strikingly alike. A survey of the front pages of fifty newspapers on the same day has shown that the decisions about the relative importance of news items made by these editors were substantially alike. Even the major exception was a consensus; some editors believe that any local story outranks a national or international event unless it is a major one. Television news editors arrange their program schedules in the same way, and again, their judgments vary little from one to the other as far as international and national news is concerned, and their decisions are substantially the same as the newspaper editors'.

A necessary personal characteristic for people who want to go into the editorial side of newspaper work is the ability to use the English language. This may seem obvious, but a common complaint of editors today about the young recruits they take on is their inability to spell and their ignorance of grammar. Not everyone who goes into the newspaper business has the same writing ability as far as style is concerned, but a reasonable minimum qualification for everybody would be an ability to use the language correctly. An editor may suffer through a recruit's training period while he improves himself, if he has other qualifications that make him promising; however, sloppy writing will not be tolerated for long on any paper except those in such financial condition that they will hire anyone they can get who will work for the lowest of salaries.

It goes without saying that the ability to type is mandatory, and while there are still veterans in the business who do it by the hunt-and-peck method, there is no reason why anyone today

Newspaper interns learn firsthand about the coordination of reporting, editorial, and production activities.

shouldn't learn the touch system. If you don't want to take the time in school and if you have your own typewriter at home, you can learn to type fifty or sixty words a minute in six weeks by using a typewriting instruction book and practicing a minimum of two hours a day. Spelling and grammar can be learned at home, too, with the aid of instruction books. Don't believe those who say of spelling, "Don't worry, not everyone can spell." Everyone *can* spell if he wants to make the effort, and similarly, he can master grammar. But there are no easy shortcuts; it takes the drudgery of drill work.

Style is another matter. The ability to write well and distinctively takes talent to begin with, and some people are better writers than others. They are the ones who presumably will get the best writing jobs, but there are thousands of newswriters who are no more than professionally competent, and that in itself is something to be proud of. Most people involved with writing are in love with words and what can be done with them. The most talented learn the routines of newswriting quickly, become highly competent in them, and go on to more specialized kinds of work on newspapers, often leaving after a time to write books or magazine articles.

Editors and copyeditors on newspapers, who process what other people have written, are not necessarily writers themselves, but many of them, perhaps most, have been reporters. Occasionally one finds someone whose training has been entirely academic. A person with a Ph.D. in English literature may end up working on the copydesk of a metropolitan newspaper, where he will be in a position to improve the use of the language by the paper's reporters.

People who like to work with words are almost invariably readers. Those who work on the editorial side of newspapers are usually well read, and their tastes in reading often are broad. They have a good background in history, especially American political, social, and cultural history, and know something about the other broad areas of human affairs. In fact, for newspaper writers, or writers in any other field for that matter, it is impossible to know too much.

There was a time when every reporter had to be a generalist if he meant to work out of a city room because he never knew when he came into the office where he might be sent. The assignment might be to interview a scientist or a movie star; to cover a murder or a banquet; to mix with the very rich or the very poor. On large metropolitan dailies today, the trend is toward specialization. At the New York *Times,* for example, the city room staff is a community of specialists, although most of these specialists could work in many other fields if it were required. On small papers, however, the general assignment reporter is still the rule. He may sell advertising, supervise the paper's make-up, and handle classified advertising, among his other jobs.

On these smaller papers, another requirement is physical endurance. Most large dailies have contracts with the American

Newspaper Guild specifying, among other things, the hours reporters and other staff members can work—usually the standard eight-hour day, five-day week; no such limits exist on the non-union papers. They work until the paper gets out, whenever that is, and stay with an assignment until the story is covered. Even on a weekly paper, there is enough to do to keep people busy six days a week and often parts of the seventh.

Not everyone who goes into the newspaper business stays in it, but on the editorial side, there is probably less attrition than in most other occupations. That is because another characteristic of the newspaperman is his dedication to what he's doing. In old movies about the newspaper business, there was often a senti-mental old editor, or an idealistic young reporter, who talked about his devotion to "the newspaper game" with tears in his eyes. There was a grain of truth in this kind of melodrama. Nobody now calls it "the newspaper game," if they ever did; and tears were probably never shed for it. But there are thousands of newspaper men and women working today who could conceive of no other way of living.

The urge to find out what's happening, then to translate it into words that will explain or illuminate the event, is something that never dies in the true newspaperman's psychic make-up. Even those who drift into related occupations in search of more money, power, or independence think of themselves in the words of that immortal cliche, "I was a newspaperman once myself," even though they are too sophisticated to say it.

These are the people who watch a live public event on television, or see a police car race by, sirens wailing, or watch the flames leaping from a burning building, or read about a sensational crime, and respond almost instinctively. "The old fire-horse hears the bell," it was once said of those retired animals who started up when they heard the sound of an alarm calling out the mechanized equipment that had replaced them. So it is with former newspapermen; so it is with present newspapermen whose lives are largely made up of public rather than private events.

Like the Army, newspapering also requires people who are characteristically patient. There is a great deal of "hurry up and wait" in newspaper work. For every intensely interesting and important assignment, there are dozens of others that are boringly routine, and countless hours are spent in city rooms waiting for something to happen on dull nights and Sundays.

A journalism student who had been warned about this before graduation asked his instructor what he should do to fortify himself, having accepted the 6 p.m. to 3 a.m. shift in the Woonsocket bureau of the Providence, Rhode Island, *Journal.* "You might try reading Dickens," the professor said. The graduate took him seriously, and a year later he wrote to say that he was being transferred into the main office but had meanwhile managed to read the British master's entire works.

Finally, among the shared characteristics of newspaper people, is a kind of generalized ability to get along with others, or at least to be the kind of person other people will talk to readily. Part of this is an art which can be learned from experience, but it is also a matter of personality. People who are shy and withdrawn, who find it hard to speak with others and especially to talk about anything that goes beyond everyday commonplaces, are not usually good reporters. I once knew a reporter who could cry at will, and if, for example, he was required to get information from a woman who had just lost her husband, he could sit down and seem to share her grief, meanwhile jotting down between sobs whatever she was able to tell him.

Such talents are certainly not required, but generally speaking, the best reporters are those who are able to persuade other people to talk to them whether they really want to or not. Knowing what questions to ask is something that can be learned through experience and through training in a good journalism school or department.

Since the newspaper profession, like any other, is composed of a large assortment of many kinds of people, it should be understood that all the personal qualifications discussed here are not possessed by everyone in the business. As on George Orwell's animal farm, some are more equal than others. But those who rise to the top seem to do so by capitalizing on their best qualities and by learning to improve on the others. The inquisitive, intellectually curious young person will learn how to conquer his impatience and overcome shyness or some other problem he may have in dealing with other people.

Those who are thinking of newspaper work as a career should also realize that reporting is by no means the only job to which they can aspire. There are those whose talent and interests lie in working with other people's words, or who have acquired expertise in sports, or music, or books, or some other activity with which newspapers deal in a specialized way. These people may never cover a fire, see the inside of a police station, or follow a politician on the campaign trail, but they nevertheless become successful members of a newspaper's staff.

In the opinion of many who have spent their lives in the newspaper business, the entire matter of career choice in this field comes down to the idea with which this opening chapter began—selection of newspaper work as a way of life, not just a job. Since Carl Bernstein and Bob Woodward achieved instant fame and glamour as the Washington *Post* reporters who broke the Watergate story, journalism schools have been thronged with applicants who want the excitement of investigative reporting and who see newspapering as something romantic, as it has not been viewed since the 1920s. Journalism is not particularly romantic, however, and its investigative function is only one aspect of the work. Those who read *All The President's Men* and saw the movie with sufficient perception will realize that a great deal of what Woodward and Bernstein did was unromantic, slogging, often unrewarding, hard work. The glamour came later.

If the student contemplating newspaper life understands that and knows that the perennial fascination of newspaper life lies in always being close to what's happening, whatever that may be; sees himself as the observer of events; and finds any other way of life inconceivable, he is a prime candidate for the field. For some, other ways of living *do* become conceivable, and people do leave newspapers for magazines, broadcasting, book publishing, or public relations, but they almost always carry with them some of that feeling for journalism. Those who stay never lose it, especially if they spend their lives working for morning newspapers and become night people. They work for newspapers because to do anything else would seem hopelessly dull.

Ask yourself if you fit this pattern and find out how you really feel about newspapering. Then consider the other qualifications we've discussed. If you've already said a resounding and emphatic "yes" to that first question, the others don't matter as much. You're committed—you're on the way to becoming a newspaperman.

CHAPTER 2

SOMETHING ABOUT THE
HISTORY OF NEWSPAPERS

"Something about" newspaper history is the correct phrase here, I think, because the few pages of this chapter can only begin to suggest the gaudy, fascinating, important, and sometimes incredible history of the American press. In the reading list at the end of this book, you'll find titles that will lead you to the whole story in detail.

The idea of the newspaper is as old as ancient Rome, where the events of each day were published in a scroll called the *Acta Diurna,* roughly "the acts of the day." That was the first newspaper of any kind. It was an idea taken up by the financial houses of middle Europe, whose far-flung interests in other parts of the world were kept informed of each other's doings and the thoughts of the home office by means of circulating newsletters. After Gutenberg invented the printing press in the fifteenth century, books and eventually newspapers of a sort began to be published in France and England.

Newspapers originated in America with the issuing of *Publick Occurrences Both Foreign and Domestick* in 1690, the work of a recently arrived English printer named Benjamin Harris. It was suppressed by the authorities after a single issue, not because it contained stories offensive to the government, although that was the case, but because it had no license to print. The Crown required licensing of printing presses, a rule wholeheartedly supported by the colonial civil and religious authorities who understood that these machines could spread ideas that might overthrow the ruling powers unless they were controlled. They were also valuable as spreaders of propaganda for the civil authorities and propagators of the faith for the religious leaders.

The authorities were not defied successfully until almost the eve of the Revolution. By that time, religious dissenters like Roger Williams had made it clear that one faith would not prevail, and civil dissenters had discovered that the press could be used as a propaganda weapon for more than one side. Consequently, the newspapers of the colonies became a valuable instrument for spreading the idea of protest and eventual independence from Britain. The Tories had their own newspapers, but they were outnumbered by those in the hands of the dissenters. The truth was not to be found in either camp; both used the papers as propaganda machines. The patriot papers were extremely useful, however, in binding together the far-flung colonists, who by this time had moved westward some distance from the port cities of the East Coast, where the struggle that was to end in open conflict had centered.

With the American nation established, the former colonists sat down to write the new rules by which it would be governed, that is, the Constitution. The delegates who met in Philadelphia assumed that the document they produced guaranteed the freedoms they had fought for, but when it was printed in the newspapers before the new states met in conventions to ratify it, a great outcry arose. It was clear that the people did not think the language of the Constitution was enough. Primary liberties were not guaranteed specifically, they said, particularly freedom of the press. Older people remembered that it was the press that had exposed the iniquities of the Crown's authorities, had inspired the people to take their courage in hand and revolt, and had kept them informed of what was happening during the long, hard years of the Revolution itself.

The result of this grassroots revolt was the Bill of Rights, put forward in the ratifying conventions and passed on to Congress, which accepted ten of the twelve proposals made. Foremost among them was the First Amendment, guaranteeing freedom of speech and the press. The language of that amendment made it perfectly clear what was intended: "Congress shall make *no* law," it said, that would abridge freedom of speech or the press, and if Congress could not make one, surely this freedom could not be abridged by anyone else, since Congress presumably spoke for the people.

To appreciate fully what this declaration meant, it is necessary to remember that the press which was being protected bore little resemblance to the one we know today. It was operating in a period often called the Dark Ages of Journalism, because the newspapers had fallen into the hands of the rival political parties, the Federalists of Washington and Hamilton, and the Anti-Federalists of Jefferson. No attempt was made to report news objectively, and the papers themselves were used by politicians to attack the other side, often in the most vicious terms, of a kind which would make today's political editorials or columns seem mild and inoffensive. Men like Washington and Jefferson were accused of the worst crimes by the opposition papers. Yet the people were intent on passing an Amendment to the Constitution that would guarantee the right of these newspapers to tell the worst lies without fear of government suppression. President John Adams tried suppression in the new Republic by his support of the infamous Alien and Sedition Acts and thereby wrecked the Federalist party, ensuring Jefferson's rise to power.

Jefferson himself was a firm believer in the First Amendment. The newspapers attacked him as scurrilously as they had his predecessors, but he made no move to suppress them. When the Prussian minister, waiting in an outer office to see him one morning, read a particularly violent attack on the President in a Federalist paper, the diplomat carried the paper into the office and cried out indignantly, "Mr. President, why do you permit such things? Why don't you have this paper suppressed and its editor punished?"

"Put that paper in your pocket, Baron," Jefferson replied, "and should you ever hear the reality of our liberty, the freedom of the press questioned, show them this paper—and tell them where you found it."

James Madison, who was the chief architect of the First Amendment, found his belief in it tested even more severely after he became President. In the War of 1812, with the British threatening to win the conflict and extinguish the new nation before it had barely begun, Madison faced a press which not only opposed what was an unpopular war, but actually advocated New England's secession from the Union. That cry was echoed on his very doorstep by an opposition newspaper in Georgetown, the *Federal Republican,* whose bitter assaults on him and on the war effort raised for the first time a troublesome question still with us today: How far should press criticism go when the country's security is threatened by an enemy?

Madison's answer to that question was a firm refusal to censor the press for any reason. He was profoundly shocked when some of his supporters destroyed the *Republican's* buildings and presses, killed one of its staff members, James Lingan, and maimed for life another, "Light Horse Harry" Lee, both former generals and heroes of the Revolution.

As long as control of the press remained in the hands of political parties, nothing much could be expected of it. The news was becoming more and more important, but not much effort was made to collect it, and even less to make sure it was accurate.

Then, in 1835, the newspaper business was revolutionized by a single individual, James Gordon Bennett, Sr., a tall, slim, eccentric Scotsman who had come to America penniless, worked on several papers from Boston to Savannah, and at last, started his own New York *Herald* with a borrowed $500, printing it in a Wall Street basement on an old press with battered type and doing all the reporting himself.

The *Herald* and Bennett transformed newspapering. Bennett showed America and the world how to get the news. As he quickly became successful, he organized the city room of his paper in much the same way it is today, established foreign correspondents whose dispatches were taken from incoming vessels by Bennett's fast packets off New York harbor and rushed to the city room, set up the first Washington bureau, and employed the newly invented telegraph to get the news first from everywhere the lines reached. Now the news ranked first in importance, not politics; Bennett did not hesitate to be political, but he did it primarily on his editorial page. The paper's coverage of business, the courts, and New York's social life was not guaranteed to be objective, but it was far removed from the recent past, when little, if any, effort was exerted to get the facts straight, or to present them fairly.

Bennett soon had extremely able rivals. Six years after the *Herald* appeared, Horace Greeley started the New York *Tribune.* This eccentric, amiable man with his floppy white hat, moon face, and squeaky voice was soon the most influential editor in America, and the *Tribune* was being read all over the country. Its influence was particularly great among the farmers, who did not care that it might be weeks late before they had a chance to read it. Greeley was the first great liberal editor. His paper was a continuing crusader for the ordinary citizen, who was beginning to struggle against the evils of both uncontrolled government and unregulated business. Greeley fought to improve both and died of a broken heart in 1872 when the common people he thought believed in him refused to make him President.

A third major paper came to New York in 1851 when Henry J. Raymond founded the New York *Times* with the help of a business partner, George Jones. It was Raymond's idea to start a nonpartisan paper, and he set down the philosophy that would guide it thereafter: "We do not mean to write as if we were in a passion—unless that shall really be the case, and we shall make it a point to get into a passion as rarely as possible." Those were strange words, coming at a time when the country was beginning to be torn apart by the issue of slavery, but Raymond stood by them, even when he himself became a partisan politician and served the party of Lincoln.

All these New York papers, and others that were springing up everywhere in the country, benefited from the Civil War, as far as circulation was concerned. For the first time, readers were able to read about a war in daily newspapers as it progressed. Reporters were on the battlefields, traveling with the armies, seeing the conflict at first hand, and reporting the details and the casualties to people waiting anxiously at home. Artists accompanied them, setting up their easels on the combat fields and reproducing the scenes of conflict in woodcuts that appeared in both newspapers and magazines like *Harper's Weekly,* which rivaled and sometimes surpassed newspaper coverage.

Dissenting newspapers in the North were known as the copperhead press if they favored the South. But there were many Northern papers that attacked Lincoln in a savage way reminiscent of the manner in which Jefferson and Washington had been assaulted. Lincoln had mixed feelings about the press. He was well aware that his nomination would not have been possible without it, particularly the Chicago *Tribune's* editors, Joseph Medill and Charles Ray, who had manipulated the convention to get him nominated. The President also, during the war, followed the papers closely and depended on them for news, seeking out correspondents returning from the front who could give him fresh information.

On the other hand, no President since Washington and Jefferson had been compelled to endure so much abuse from the press, and there were only two or three major papers he could depend on. Like his famous predecessors, however, Lincoln refused to suppress newspapers, even the copperhead press. Suppression was sometimes taken out of his hands by military commanders who would not tolerate local opposition and even less the uncensored dispatches of reporters in the field, known as "specials." General Sherman was particularly angry and arbitrary in his treatment of the press. He once had one of Greeley's reporters arrested as a spy and would have had him shot if Lincoln had not intervened.

The war displayed the newspaper in a new role. Its importance before had been as an instrument of dissent. In the war against Mexico in 1846, it had opposed this unpopular conflict as it had the War of 1812, and while it had not persuaded a stubborn President Polk to end it, so much public pressure was generated that the peace terms were much less harsh than the President would like to have imposed. In the Civil War, the newspapers had served as a great debating platform before the conflict and, once it had begun, were unifying forces in both the North and the South. But on both sides, too, the press now emerged as a prime source of information, of news, and so it remained.

After the war, the newspaper business boomed as it never had before. Major papers appeared in other parts of the country besides New York and Chicago. In the South, Henry W. Grady preached reconciliation and the dream of a New South in his Atlanta *Constitution,* while in Louisville, "Marse Henry" Watterson, looking like the traditional stereotype of the Kentucky Colonel, pursued the same theme with what would be the *Courier-Journal.* The concept of community service as the newspaper's function was the basis of Victor Lawson's Chicago *Daily News* and of William Rockhill Nelson's Kansas City *Star,* which vowed to "pull Kansas City out of the mud" and did. In the Far West, flamboyant journalism reflecting that raw and growing region was practiced on the Denver *Post* and on the San Francisco papers.

In New York, more journalistic giants appeared on the scene. Charles Anderson Dana, who had interrupted his career as Greeley's managing editor to serve in Lincoln's war cabinet, returned to New York and bought the decrepit *Sun,* which he soon made into one of the country's best newspapers. The *Sun* originated, or at least perfected, the human interest (feature) story, and its staff of talented writers produced a flood of stories which mirrored the human life of the city. Its city editor, John Bogart, coined a famous definition of news: "If a dog bites a man, that's not news; if a man bites a dog, that's news." One of its accomplished editorial writers, Francis Church, wrote a line that is still a part of our common speech, "Yes, Virginia, there is a Santa Claus."

Dana's chief rivals were now James Gordon Bennett, Jr., the even more eccentric son of an eccentric father, and Joseph Pulitzer. Bennett, Sr. had shown how to get the news and get it first; his son demonstrated how to make the news. His most memorable feat was to send Henry Stanley, a London reporter, to find David Livingstone, a missionary explorer presumably lost in the African bush. The meeting of these two men produced another quotation still embedded in the language, "Dr. Livingstone, I presume," to which the missionary answered, "Yes." Bennett left New York in a rage after a bizarre scandal and thereafter ran his newspaper from his favorite country, France, or from his yacht, becoming increasingly more eccentric as he grew older.

Joseph Pulitzer's eccentricity was of a different kind, apparently a neurological disturbance that made him acutely sensitive to noise, a condition that worsened in time and undermined his health until he was nearly blind, compelling him to spend much of his time at sea on his yacht, from which he, too, ran his paper. That paper, the New York *World,* nevertheless became the foremost journal in America between the Civil War and the end of the century. Pulitzer did everything his predecessors and rivals had done, and he usually did it better. His crusading, liberal editorials were reminders of Greeley at his best. Coverage of the news was as well written as the *Sun's* and as diversified as the *Herald's.* He was the first publisher to produce a Sunday paper, which was filled with some of the best newspaper writing of the day.

Pulitzer's supremacy was challenged in 1892 by a brash upstart from California, William Randolph Hearst, the first publisher of a major paper who had started out rich instead of working his way up from the bottom. Hearst's father, George, had accumulated a fortune from his gold and silver mines and had become a United States Senator. His mother, a gentle woman named Phoebe, had raised her son with an appreciation of art and a knowledge of the better things in life. As soon as he began to read Pulitzer's *World* while he was still a student at Harvard, he determined that publishing such a paper was the only career for him.

Dropping out of Harvard after his sophomore year, he persuaded his father to give him the San Francisco *Examiner,* a dying paper which the Senator had once bought for political purposes, and transformed it into a West Coast version of the *World,* but going Pulitzer one better in daring innovation and flamboyant treatment of the news. When he had launched it successfully, he went to New York and started a replica of the *Examiner* which he called the *Journal.* Soon he was engaged in a life-and-death struggle with Pulitzer and the *World* for dominance.

It was an unfair contest. Pulitzer was ill and aging. Hearst was young and rich and had nothing to lose. He hired away many of Pulitzer's best people and proceeded to outdo the *World* in nearly every respect. His Sunday paper was bigger, better, and more outrageous. He hired Pulitzer's best cartoonist, Richard Outcault, and encouraged him to create a feature called "The Yellow Kid," which marked the birth of the comic strip in America. Money was no object. He could command the best talent, and he did.

The climax of this struggle came with the Spanish-American War. Hearst and Pulitzer clamored for the United States to enter it, leading a nationwide journalistic chorus which crystallized public sentiment and pushed a reluctant President McKinley into the conflict. Hearst has been given credit for starting the war, but he was only the loudest voice in the chorus that demanded it, going to such lengths that his enemies called what he did "yellow journalism," another phrase still in the language—derived, of course, from Outcault's Yellow Kid, whose costume was printed in yellow ink, the first use of color in a newspaper.

With the entry of American forces into Cuba, Hearst and Pulitzer transferred their competition to covering the war. Hearst bought an old freighter, put a printing press and type in its hold, and sent it down to Cuba with a load of reporters and photographers. The reporters were often in the front line with the troops, and the paper's chief correspondent was wounded at the battle of El Caney. He recovered consciousness to find Hearst himself bending over him with notebook in hand, waiting to get his verbal report.

Pulitzer was less enterprising and less financially able to match his rival. At the end of the war, he gave up the struggle to compete, turned his paper to better things, and after his death in 1910, the *World* became one of the great newspapers of the world—"the newspaperman's newspaper," as it was often called—until its demise in 1930. Pulitzer left behind something more lasting, however—the prizes which he established in his name and the School of Journalism at Columbia University.

As for Hearst, his spectacular career only began to approach a climax in the first years of the twentieth century. He continued to buy newspapers, establishing the first chain of them (multiple ownerships, as we say now), and buying other properties, including magazines in both England and the United States. Hearst's newspaper properties were hard hit by the Great Depression and diminished to the relative few which survive today, but his magazine empire, most notably *Good House-keeping* and *Cosmopolitan,* continue to flourish. Hearst's personal and political life were often in the headlines. In politics, he swung from far left to far right during his career, and consequently, he made a good many enemies on both sides of the fence. His newspapers were often removed from libraries and clubs or attacked in other ways; before America's entry into the first

World War, he was believed to be a German spy. Hearst survived everything until he died in 1952, still rich and famous.

The turn of the century and the decade or so that followed it marked a significant turning point in American journalistic history. The death of the old giants like the Bennetts, Dana, and Pulitzer left only Hearst as the remaining highly individual publisher, with a few lesser exceptions like E. W. Scripps, the self-styled "damned old crank" who founded the Scripps-Howard chain. Newspapers had begun as political propaganda organs, became the personal enterprises of strong-minded, highly publicized publishers with the advent of Bennett Sr., and now were turning into business enterprises whose publishers were less colorful and increasingly not even recognizable to the general public.

There was a good reason for this change. When advertising began to replace circulation as the chief support of newspaper properties, the interests of the publishers became much more identical with those of the business community. Circulation was still important, but it was not a paper's sole or major support any longer, and the competitive drive to get it which had inspired the Bennetts, Pulitzer, Hearst, and the others was considerably reduced. True, there were great circulation wars in the Chicago of the 1920s and in New York as well, but the overall long-term trend was toward the development of local and national advertising revenues.

As business institutions, increasingly run by businessmen, newspapers lost much of the glamour the giants of the nineteenth century had given them, but they gained something else, something more important. The newspaper was now no longer the tool of either a political party or an individual entrepreneur, and so it could approach the news from a much more impartial standpoint. Sometimes it erred on the opposite side, protecting the interests of the business world, of which it was a vital part. On the whole, however, newspapers of this century made great strides toward the impossible ideal of objectivity. By comparison with everything that had gone before, the American press, generally, had become as fair and accurate as fallible humans could make it.

The Great Depression reduced the number of newspapers, but the press survived to become healthier than ever with the coming of World War II. The rise of tabloids in the 1920s, beginning with the New York *Daily News,* already had given a new dimension to journalism. The *News,* with its comic strips, sex and scandal, colloquial editorials, and its overall effort to reach a mass audience, had become the newspaper with the largest circulation in the country. Its circulation and that of every paper boomed during the vast global war, as the press used all of the new technology that had appeared since World War I to report a conflict more thoroughly and accurately than had ever been done before.

It was a last hurrah for newspapers in the area of hard news coverage. Even before Pearl Harbor, David Sarnoff, the president of RCA, had made the first public television broadcast at the New York World's Fair of 1939. When the war was over, the television broadcasting industry burst into full bloom; by 1950, it was beginning to challenge the dominance of the print media.

It has been challenging ever since, but the newspaper has far from disappeared, as some media seers predicted when television first began to saturate the mass audience. Similar predictions about the doom of all the print media had been made as early as the 1890s, when suddenly all America appeared to be riding on bicycles and it was seriously believed that no one would stay home to read any more. The doomsayers repeated their warnings with the successive popularity of the automobile, motion pictures and radio, but the print media continued not only to co-exist but to continue their own expansion.

Not that television has made no difference. The big city daily has been declining slowly for some time, since television took away the spot news function which had always been its great strength. Other factors, primarily the decay of the central city, have also been at work. But there has been a corresponding upsurge in suburban dailies and weeklies, and the newspaper business continues to grow in other directions. Another change has been the newspaper's development of background and investigative material to replace the spot news function it has lost. In this effort, it must compete with magazines, many of which have also been moving in that direction, so that today the line between newspapers and magazines is much less distinct, as far as editorial content is concerned, than it once was. Together, they do what television cannot do on any comparable scale, at least as the industry is presently constituted.

Newspapers are still changing, as we'll see in later chapters, but now primarily because new technology is changing them. In the lifetimes of those who are presently thinking about careers in journalism, the whole organization of papers and the methods of delivering them to readers may change radically. The press has come a great way from Ben Harris's ill-fated *Publick Occurrences.* As an American institution, its strength rests uniquely in the First Amendment, which separates the press of this country from the remainder of the world. No press is more free, and none in the Western world is under attack from so many different sources. But only its worst enemies doubt that it is the kingpin in the freedom which our system of government enjoys, the buffer zone between the governors and the governed.

CHAPTER 3

THE SCOPE OF NEWSPAPER WORK

Newspapers are the least diversified of any communications medium, although the companies or corporations that publish papers may also own magazines, radio and television stations, book publishing houses, or any number of other businesses wholly unrelated to the media. For career purposes, it is more convenient here to talk about newspapers alone, remembering that those who go to work for a large communications complex, beginning on a newspaper, may wind up in some other part of the forest.

STRINGERS

To begin at the lowest rung of the ladder, stringers, those often unsung correspondents who work by themselves on space rates, have offered what may be the most common approach to getting into the newspaper business, at least for generations of writers. There is, of course, a hierachy in the stringer system. At the bottom is the young man or woman still in high school who writes school news for the local paper, sometimes without pay if the local editor is not above exploiting them. They may, at the same time, write local news items after school hours, thus working themselves into summer jobs on the paper.

If they happen to be doing this in small towns which have a county seat paper nearby, they can begin sending in town news, for which they will be paid so much per column inch for everything the editor uses. These rural papers usually carry columns of "locals," as they are called, meaning short-paragraph social items—"Millie Jones visited her grandmother, Mrs. Ada Jones, last weekend. Her mother, Mrs. Horace Jones, of South Doodad, will be joining her next week."

Not very inspiring as a start in the business, after seeing or reading *All The President's Men,* true, but for many thousands of young Americans, it has been the gateway to better things. Once established in an area, the stringer can try sending in items to larger dailies in the state which run what are called "state pages," carrying news items from small towns in the paper's circulation area. If the area happens to be a lively one for news, this kind of reporting can be built into a small business, whereby the stringers may be getting income from a half-dozen state dailies, or more. The financial rewards are not great, but they may help out in paying college expenses. The job also provides extremely valuable basic reporting experience, as well as training in writing, particularly if the stringer reads his work carefully when it appears in print to see what the copyeditors have done with it.

It ought to be pointed out that this approach to the business is considerably easier in some states than others. Obviously, in a large Western state where there are relatively fewer papers, it is more difficult to become a stringer than in Ohio or Michigan, let's say. But in every state there is at least one bureau of the Associated Press and United Press International, the two major American wire services; stringers are the lifeblood of these organizations, feeding into the bureau offices news from places which would otherwise not be covered. That is how something of interest that happens in an obscure town in Wyoming, for instance, may be reported next day in the New York *Times* and in newspapers all over the country. Some stringer has covered the story and sent it to a wire service bureau, which in turn has put it on the wire to New York headquarters, where it is distributed to all the service's clients.

SMALL TOWN PAPERS

Stringing is indeed the bottom rung of newspaper work, but it's a place to learn and a means of getting started. The next step is often a job in the next layer of newspaper organization, the small town paper. They have proliferated since the advent of the photo-offset press, which makes it possible to start a newspaper for a fraction of what it once cost. Of these more than 8,000 small town papers, so many are weeklies that the whole field tends to be called by that name. In reality, however, there are biweeklies, triweeklies, and even semimonthlies. Some are tabloids, others come in odd sizes like those on the islands of Nantucket and Martha's Vineyard, which are wider than the others; most, however, are the same standard size as their big city counterparts. Many are small and struggling, getting by on 8 or 16 pages a week. Others regularly run 36 pages or more, and some large suburban weeklies have a hundred or more pages.

As America has become a country in which 80 percent of the people live in cities or in the suburbs that ring them, the big metropolitan dailies have been in a slow decline, while the surrounding weeklies have gained in number and affluence. These suburban papers are primarily advertising media, but they also serve as community bulletin boards. In the small towns outside metropolitan circulation zones, the weeklies not only serve as bulletin boards but also record the life of the town in a way that big newspapers cannot do, even with the best of local coverage.

The chief rival of the weekly is likely to be the local shopper's guide, by whatever name it happens to be called. These are actually advertising media, but the columns breaking up the ads to prevent them from running solidly are filled with syndicated material called "boiler plate" and occasionally, with a pretense at local news coverage (mostly of the bulletin board variety)—church services, club announcements, and the like.

DAILY NEWSPAPERS

One step above the weekly is a less diversified and more homogeneous group, the daily newspaper, of which there are about 1,750 in the United States. These papers range all the way from the prestigious New York *Times* to dailies in towns as small as 5,000 population, or less. But whatever the size of the community they serve, dailies have not only their regularity of publication in common, but they have, generally speaking, the same format. The mavericks in the group stand out.

The two major differences are whether they are morning or afternoon newspapers, and whether they are tabloid or full size, meaning the eight-column paper with which we are all familiar. All dailies operate around the clock with at least some kind of staff, but the morning papers concentrate their work from late afternoon to early morning and appear on the street and on their readers' doorsteps either sometime during the late evening or very early the next morning. Afternoon papers concentrate their efforts from early morning until sometime in mid-afternoon. Their editions usually begin appearing about 10:30 a.m., with finals in early or mid-afternoon—in any case, not too late to catch the outward flow of commuters.

America is a nation of morning paper readers. Nearly all of the best daily journals are in that category. Traditionally, afternoon papers are more lively in their news coverage, seeking to entertain more than instruct the homegoing commuter or the person who picks up the paper after dinner. A large part of the information in afternoon papers is in the financial section, particularly closing prices on the stock exchanges.

Tabloid journalism began as a deliberate attempt to reach mass audiences at the lower educational and social levels with what it was presumed they wanted to read—that is, scandal, sports, plenty of pictures, gossip and other columns, all of it cast in a more or less sensational tone. On that premise, the New York

Daily News, first and most successful of the major tabloids, established itself as the most widely read paper in America. The *News* still retains something of its original flavor, but like the others, it has become much more sober as tabloid journalism has taken on a different meaning. Some newspapers have reduced themselves to tabloid size for economic reasons, others believe that reader convenience is almost as valid a reason for tabloidism. In any case, major tabloids like the Chicago *Sun-Times,* for example, are no longer like the flamboyant, sex-and-scandal sheets of the 1920s in New York and Chicago, but simply standard newspapers in a smaller format.

Wire Services. An important part of the American press structure, as I've indicated in talking about stringers, are the wire services. They supplement the newsgathering organizations of the papers themselves, sometimes supplying news from places geographically beyond a staff's coverage, at other times supplementing that coverage. The New York *Times,* for example, with the largest foreign and domestic newsgathering staff in the world, nevertheless uses not only the two major American wire services, but the British, French, and several others. Not even the *Times* reporters can cover everything.

For daily papers which are not financially able to afford their own foreign staffs, or even correspondents in other American cities, the wire services are indispensable. Some major newspapers like the New York *Times,* the Washington *Post,* and .the Los Angeles *Times* have their own wire services, selling the work of their columnists and reporters to other papers, some as far away as the *International Herald Tribune,* in Paris.

Syndication. Syndication is another facet of the newspaper business. Large syndicates like United Features and King Features sell everything from comic strips to political columns, household hints, advice to the lovelorn columns, and, in fact, columns covering nearly all areas of human activity. A single columnist may be printed in 600 newspapers or more as a result of syndication. A popular comic strip like "Peanuts" may reach newspapers all over the world through the syndicate.

There are also picture syndicates, some of them adjuncts of other organizations, like the Associated Press Wide World; others are independent suppliers of photographs coming from many sources. The AP pioneered in the transmission of pictures by wire, now a regular feature in the news rooms of large papers.

Group Journals. In terms of business organization, the most striking development of this century has been the spread of what was once known as chain journalism. The owners now prefer to call them "groups" or "multiple ownerships," to avoid criticism of them as monolithic, or monopolies. These groups are, in truth, not monopolies, since they compete with each other, and not always monolithic in the sense that they have no individual autonomy. Early group owners like Hearst and the Scripps-Howard interests did put their own stamp on papers, however. All the papers in each of these groups looked more or less alike typographically, and while each individual editor was given individual autonomy over the operation of his paper, subject to firing or transfer, financial and business policy emanated from the top. Moreover, editorials were sent to all the papers from a central headquarters. In the Hearst group, these were often written by Hearst himself and no editor would refuse to print them. In the Scripps-Howard group, the essays came from a chief editorial writer in Washington, and while individual editors nominally had the power to reject them, the occasion did not often arise.

Today editorial control from the top is considerably looser in one sense. Editors have more autonomy and try to shape their papers to community needs. However, papers in a group do not differ from each other politically, and since these chains are all large business enterprises, it is not surprising that they are all conservative in their politics. Scripps-Howard and Hearst papers still tend to look alike, but others, like the newspapers in the

From reporter on the street to delivery on your doorstep, a newspaper requires the services of many skilled personnel.

Newhouse group, make no attempt to enforce conformity of appearance.

A single exception to the general pattern are the papers which were owned by Roy Thomson, the Canadian who became the world's foremost press lord (and Lord Thomson in his own right) by first buying the leading papers in Scotland and England, then expanding his empire into magazines, book publishing houses, radio and television stations, travel agencies, and even an airline. The Thomson holdings are in the United Kingdom, the United States, Africa, Asia, the West Indies, and a scattered few elsewhere. Thomson, who died in 1976, was the largest owner of newspapers in America, having bought whole groups at once; he owned no major newspapers in this country, however. Lord Thomson exercised complete financial control over his properties, but his editors have enjoyed complete autonomy so far as the papers' contents are concerned. Thomson did not care what they did editorially, as long as they met the needs of the community, and he saw no contradiction in his ownership of a segregationist newspaper in the American South and his joint ownership with blacks of newspapers in Africa.

Group journalism is increasing in the United States because of rising costs in newspaper operation; obviously, it is more economical to spread those costs over several newspapers. Even competing newspapers in some cities—San Francisco, for example—have found it a financial lifesaver to combine some of their business operations, retaining the independence of the editorial and advertising departments. To those who see increasing monopoly in all these developments, newspaper owners point out that the alternative is fewer newspapers as individual journals succumb to cost factors.

NEWSPAPER ORGANIZATIONS

As an industry, newspapers are highly organized. The American Newspaper Publishers Association is the primary organization of owners, while editorial executives may join the American Society of Newspaper Editors. The states have their own press associations, and there are various regional groupings like the Inland Press Association, as well as such international organizations as the Inter-American Press Association and the International Press Institute, both of which have American members. There are also, of course, all kinds of local press clubs.

The Society of Professional Journalists, until recently known as Sigma Delta Chi, has a national membership of journalists from every kind of publication and people from allied professions like public relations. Its monthly magazine, the *Quill,* is circulated among these members and others. Members also may join local clubs affiliated with the Society, attending club meetings to hear talks on professional topics. The Society has both regional conventions and an annual national assemblage.

Non-editorial segments of the business also are well organized. Circulation, promotion, and advertising people all have their own national and local organizations, each with various kinds of subsidiary affiliations.

Newspaper workers are organized into unions from top to bottom, covering every phase of their operation, from the reporters who gather the news to the pressmen who print it. The American Newspaper Guild represents editorial workers, but since it is a vertical and not a craft union, it also represents others on the business and maintenance staffs. The International Typographical Union represents the various mechanical workers through locals of the organization.

Unionization is strongest in the larger cities, weakest in the smaller ones and in small towns generally, where it is largely nonexistent. For most smaller papers, it would be economically impossible to pay anything approaching the union scales prevalent in larger communities. In the larger cities, many Guild contracts provide for closed shops, and newcomers to the organization have no choice but to join.

Of all the organizations described here, the Society of Professional Journalists may be the most helpful to those who want to get into the newspaper business. Besides the scholarships offered by many local chapters, the Society sponsors chapters in a good many colleges and universities as part of the activities of schools and departments of journalism. Students joining these chapters become members of the Society and participate in a variety of professional programs. It is a useful bridge between training for journalism and the newspaper business itself.

CHAPTER 4

SMALL TOWN WEEKLIES AND DAILIES

There is one striking difference between working for a small town weekly or daily and being on the staff of a large metropolitan paper, quite aside from the obvious difference in size. The big city reporter goes out on an assignment, covers his story, and presumably will not again see the people who made the news unless they are public officials of some kind. By contrast, the small town newspaperman not only sees the same people repeatedly, perhaps several times a week, but he may also see some of them socially and will certainly see them in restaurants, bars, in church, at sports events, or on the street. It's the difference between big city anonymity and small town togetherness.

Inevitably, this primary difference has an effect on the kind of work the reporter does—and for that matter, on the way the editor runs his paper. Small town editors often like to proclaim their independence, but few of them can make it stick. They are totally dependent on local merchants for advertising and in some cases, on local bankers for financing. An ardently liberal Democratic editor, for instance, who comes into a solidly conservative Republican community and begins crusading for left-of-center causes may well find himself in serious trouble. Organized business people in such a town can just about dictate what kind of local paper they are going to have.

As for the small town reporter, he may as well forget any dreams of becoming a junior Woodward or Bernstein. Most small town papers are not in the investigative business. Not that there is nothing to investigate. Political corruption exists in small towns as well as cities, and it would be an extremely unobservant reporter who did not encounter it in local governments, where it is likely to be entrenched in various kinds of cozy relationships. A young reporter encountering evidence of this kind of thing will be quietly discouraged from investigating further, or will be told openly to forget about it.

There are exceptions, of course. A few small town editors have made names for themselves by courageously fighting against traditional attitudes and beliefs, at considerable risk to their lives and property. We think at once of those who fought for civil liberties in the South against the segregationists and the Ku Klux Klan. Some of them later took on the John Birch Society and other extreme right-wing organizations as well. There are the reporters, too, who worked for those editors at even greater risk, perhaps, since they were the ones who were physically in the places where it was dangerous to be. Similar examples could be cited from other regions of the country, involving different issues. It's not the same thing for a newspaperman working in a town of 5,000, let's say, to carry on investigative reporting among people he sees every day as it is for the big city reporter probing into municipal corruption, unless organized crime is part of the story.

The average reporter or editor on the small town weekly or daily is not likely to encounter such situations, however. They are much more common on the next level of newspaper size—the small city daily. In a small town, life on the paper is keyed to the relatively easy pace of such a community. But no one should imagine for a moment that working on a small town weekly is an easygoing, undemanding kind of existence. On the contrary, people working on these papers put in much longer hours than their big city colleagues. There are no unions to prescribe the number of hours that may be worked; the staff simply works until they are finished, whenever that may be. Let's look at a typical week in the life of a reporter on such a newspaper.

Most weeklies are published on Thursday or Friday for an obvious reason—the big shopping days are Friday and Saturday, including Saturday night, and the advertising is keyed to that fact. Thursday night, then, is the usual deadline, which also means that the papers must come off the presses in time to meet train, bus, or whatever other kinds of transportation the paper uses in order to get its product into the circulation zone it covers.

So life begins on Monday morning for the reporter. In a great many communities, it starts in a local coffee shop, where the people who "really run the town" habitually gather. This informal backstairs government is a characteristic of small communities everywhere, and the group that meets every morning over a cup of coffee may include a banker, a lawyer, an insurance man, a department store owner, sometimes a community official—the composition of the group shifts somewhat and the same people are not always present.

There is nothing particularly sinister about these meetings. These men are simply the "old hands" in the town, the people who know what's going on by reason of their experience and their businesses. They meet out of friendship and exchange views, ideas, and gossip. A young reporter who attaches himself to such a group by virtue of his personality can learn a great deal about what is happening, or may happen, in the town simply by keeping his ears open and asking questions that don't seem to be part of his job.

A reporter can't intrude himself into such a group. He has to be accepted as one of the boys, exchanging the usual banter and wisecracks, never pushing himself or his paper. This is the kind of thing that cannot be taught in journalism schools, but comes from a feeling for other people and an acquired knowledge of how small towns work. The implication here, one must add, is that the people in these groups and the reporters themselves are men, and in fact they usually are; small towns are strongholds of male chauvinism. But an intelligent, competent woman (more chauvinism, true, but unavoidable) can often become part of this unofficial government and may succeed in being accepted without any overtones of either sex or sexism.

After coffee, the day for the reporter continues with his making the rounds of news sources. Some papers are so small that he may have to cover all the sources; others have small staffs of up to a half-dozen or so. In any case, the sources include the offices of the city government; the sheriff's office, state police, constable's office, or whatever the law enforcing units may be; the courthouse, if the town happens to be a county seat, where the offices of county officials must be covered as well as the court, if it's in session; the school superintendent's office, and the offices of any other educational institution in the town; and finally, any specialized news sources the reporter may have developed on his own.

Not all of these sources are visited every day, as the law enforcement units must be, and some of them can be covered by telephone. But if possible, the experienced small town reporter prefers to cover them in person because it is the daily chatting with the sources, face to face, that produces news. People on the telephone can put you off.

Whatever news is gathered in the morning is written that day; otherwise, the reporter will find himself submerged by his notes. It is also necessary to keep the copy moving into the composing room during the week so the same fate won't befall the compositors.

Along with the regular coverage of these news beats, the reporter will be covering whatever events may be occurring in the town, whether it is spot news like accidents or fires, or planned events like civic celebrations, speeches, or important visitors. On many small papers, a reporter may also be covering everything from sports to weddings, although the latter will probably not require his attendance, since the families are only too happy to provide material for a story.

Nothing, in fact, is outside the ken of most weekly reporters. They may have to take classified ads at the desk in the office and may even go out and sell a little advertising occasionally. They will certainly be doing some editing, not only on their own stories but on the "locals" sent in by stringers from outlying villages. Sometimes the locals come in handwritten and have to be typed; they nearly always need editing for punctuation, spelling, and grammar. The weekly reporter will usually find himself not only working on this and other copy, but also helping out in the writing of headlines.

By the time Thursday arrives, he will not only have been working all day, every day, in the routine just described, but if there are events occurring at night (sports, for example), he will have his evenings filled, too. Thursday itself is a day of intense pressure because everything that is going to be in the paper has to be written and edited against that deadline. It is not an exact deadline, as on a metropolitan daily, but a floating one, determined by the mailing schedules more than anything else.

On many weeklies, the reporter may have to be in the composing room on Thursday night, helping to supervise the make-up, standing by the composing stones to assist the compositor with the make-up, reading galley proofs and making cuts in stories so that they will fit, later reading page proofs and making last-minute corrections. When the paper is on the presses, it is not unknown for the reporter to wait and help with the delivery to the bus station, truck stop, or whatever means is being used to deliver the finished product. Only then can he go home and sleep.

Even after these exertions, unheard of for someone working on a larger paper, the week is not over. There will very probably be stories breaking on Friday, Saturday, and Sunday, particularly in sports; these are also days when the law enforcement people are likely to be especially busy. Whatever they are, these events have to be covered for next week's paper.

To anyone contemplating a career in journalism, this sounds like a strenuous seven-day week, and you may well ask what the advantages are in such labor. The answer is that working on a weekly is the best possible training ground for newspaper work, and the more you are required to do, the better. If metropolitan journalism is your goal, there are some things you will be doing on a weekly that will never be required of you later. But on the other hand, the experience gained in doing them will be useful in a thousand ways during your career.

The sheer volume of writing required from the small town reporter, and the staggering variety of it, is excellent training. For someone who is learning to write, there is no substitute for writing—the more the better, unless it's fiction. A word of caution is necessary, however. It is easy to develop bad writing habits in such situations because the standards are lower on weeklies, and there is no copydesk to improve the product. If he has the sense of craftsmanship any writer ought to have, the young reporter on a weekly will try to study good writing in larger papers and seek to improve his own; otherwise, he will simply put down whatever comes into his head first, good or bad. This is the time to develop the self-critical attitude every professional writer needs, no matter what he is writing.

Aside from the writing, weekly newspapermen get a sense of all the basic elements in the business, and a chance to try their hand at most of what it takes to put out a newspaper. This may lead to other careers. For example, many weeklies require a reporter to be a photographer as well, and if the young recruit has a talent for news photography, he will have an opportunity to discover it. In any case, this skill will be useful on larger papers, too, all the way up to those which can afford their own photographers.

There are other less tangible rewards in weekly newspapering. One is the sense of living the life of a community intensely, on a level that no one else in it can experience. To be present at all of a town's events, whatever they may be, to know more of its citizens and experience vicariously their lives and problems, to make friends at every social and economic level—all this can be an extremely satisfying experience.

The chief disadvantage is an obvious one—money. Salaries on a weekly newspaper are low for everyone by comparison with larger metropolitan papers. However, conditions are better than they used to be. A recent Newspaper Fund survey shows that the average range of newspaper salaries on weeklies is as follows:

Less than $100 a week	18.2 percent
Between $101 and $120	18.2 percent
Between $121 and $140	9.0 percent
Between $141 and $160	36.4 percent
More than $160	18.2 percent

These figures are derived from the Newspaper Fund's survey of journalism school graduates.

Most young women and men who start their newspaper careers on a weekly probably consider it as just that—an initial stage of a more ambitious career. They work until they can get a job on a larger paper, meanwhile learning everything they can. But not all are looking beyond their small town careers. Living in a small town and working on its newspaper can have a particular charm, and there are those who find that way of life delightful. Such people often make a career on a weekly, with the hope of eventually owning one. Often, the small town newspaper owner is someone who has had metropolitan experience and has returned because he prefers small town life.

Henry Beetle Hough is the best example of a newspaperman who never wanted anything more than life on a weekly. A graduate of the School of Journalism at Columbia University, he married a classmate and started the *Vineyard Gazette,* in Edgartown, Massachusetts, on Martha's Vineyard. In time, the *Gazette* became perhaps the best known weekly newspaper in

America, and Hough's books about it, *Country Editor* and *Once More The Thunderer,* are classics in their field. Through these books and his novels, Hough became a nationally known writer, but he preferred to be known as the editor of the *Gazette,* a familiar figure to all the inhabitants of the Vineyard and as much a part of its landscape as the beaches. He sold his newspaper a few years ago to James Reston, of the New York *Times,* but continued to be its guiding spirit.

There are thousands of less-celebrated Henry Houghs all over the country who have found a deep satisfaction in owning and editing country weeklies. Joseph Dennie, the eighteenth century editor who operated the first weekly of any consequence in America, in Walpole, New Hampshire, well understood these satisfactions. He liked to sit in a local tavern, talking with his friends and occasionally turning out those delightful essays which appeared in his paper, *The Farmer's Museum.* The copy was carried across the street to the composing room by Joseph Buckingham, the printer's devil (as apprentices were called), and these essays made Dennie, under his pseudonym "The Lay Preacher," one of the best known writers in America.

While that kind of pleasant newspapering disappeared long ago, something of the flavor still lingers in papers like the *Gazette* and others which are published in beautiful natural settings, or whose owners are exceptional people. The style and tone of these journals set them apart from the others. For the most part, however, weekly papers are largely routine chroniclers of small town life. Beginning newspapermen will find them a valuable training ground, and some will see in them a satisfying and permanent way of life.

CHAPTER 5

WORKING ON SMALLER CITY DAILIES

What is the difference between a small town daily and a smaller city daily, one might reasonably ask? Or between a small town weekly and daily, aside from frequency of publication?

Fair questions, but not easy to answer. When a small town weekly in a community of 5,000, let's say, turns itself into a daily, usually as the result of a population increase, certain changes take place. A wire service printer is installed to bring domestic and foreign news not previously carried, and more syndicated material is contracted. This quite often is political columns, because the paper will now more closely resemble its big city neighbors and lose some of its local flavor and bulletin board character. More staff will no doubt be added, both in the editorial and composing rooms, simply because the effort required to put out five editions a week takes more people. Adding reporters and editors means that the original staff will not have to cover so much territory individually.

But a small town daily is not transformed into a small city daily simply because a community with a population of somewhere between 25,000 and 75,000 is large enough to demand a news organization modeled much more closely on the metropolitan daily.

The distinctions between the two are unavoidably blurred, and there is a great deal of overlapping. Some small town dailies are so beautifully written and edited that they compare favorably with papers in cities of more than a million population, even though

The city editor has been called the "core of newsroom organization."

they do not carry as many pages. On the other hand, there are papers in some of the largest "small cities" which are journalistic junkpiles and would hardly do credit to any community, of any size.

Perhaps the best way to make the distinctions as clear as possible is, once more, to describe the average day of a reporter for a small city daily, providing a comparison with the routine of the weekly reporter described in the preceding chapter.

The work week of the small city daily reporter is Monday through Friday in most cases, although some of these papers are rich enough in advertising to publish a weekend edition on Saturday, designed mostly to catch Saturday shoppers. His working day will be determined by whether the paper is morning or evening, in the manner described earlier. Small city dailies tend to be afternoon papers for a variety of reasons. For one thing, they are often close enough to the circulation zone of one or more metropolitan dailies so that these papers would give them unfair competition in the morning. Then, too, afternoon papers are usually delivered by carriers late in the day so that they are read before dinner and before evening television viewing begins.

Needless to say, television news has affected these traditional patterns in morning and afternoon publication, particularly the afternoon newspapers, which find themselves competing with the local and network news shows from 6 to 7:30 p.m. Morning newspaper reading appears to be a more deeply ingrained habit, and the morning television news shows, loaded as they are with feature material, do not provide the same kind of hard news competition.

In the editorial rooms of the small city daily, the reporter finds his work much like that of all except the largest big city papers. For the first time, specialties appear. The reporter who wrote sports along with everything else on the weekly may now find himself covering them exclusively, on a sports staff that may include three or more people. There are "beats," as they are called, to be covered with a person in city hall, another in police headquarters, and another to cover federal agencies, if they are housed jointly in one building.

While big dailies have become, more and more, collections of specialists, the smaller ones have retained the pattern originated by James Gordon Bennett before the Civil War—that is, a corps of general assignment reporters. In operation, that means the reporter coming to work is available for whatever kind of assignment he may be given. The assignments for the day, or evening, may be waiting for him in his city room mailbox, or they may come directly from the city editor or his assistant.

The pleasure of general assignment reporting is its infinite variety. To come to work not knowing whether you will be sent to cover a banquet for five hundred people with a prominent speaker, to interview a visiting celebrity who may be a movie star or a scientist, to cover a fast-breaking murder story, or to attend a convention—that is a satisfying kind of day for a reporter who loves his work.

On the other hand, a certain amount of boredom can set in. There are dull news nights and days, along with the active ones. The general assignment reporter sits at his desk, literally waiting for something to happen. A conscientious city editor will not let him put in his time for long by reading other publications; he may be given some continuing story from a previous edition and asked to put a second-day lead on it. This means he will have to call the people involved to find out if anything new has happened, then rewrite the first story to present the new developments.

General assignment reporters on these smaller papers also do the rewrite work which specialists do exclusively on metropolitan dailies. The telephone on a rewrite desk is equipped with headphones, and when the city editor says, "Police beat, on number 2," the reporter puts on the headset, punches the proper button, and hears the voice of the beat man in police headquarters who gives him the facts on a story he has obtained. The rewrite man takes notes, asks to have names spelled if he's in any doubt, asks other questions, and then writes the story after he hangs up. Sometimes the beat man will have as many as four or five stories at a time, enough to keep a reporter busy for a while.

There are tales of legendary rewrite men who could compose stories on the typewriter as they heard the beat man's voice in their headsets, but most have to make do with taking notes and then writing. Much of the rewrite on both morning and afternoon papers is done during the day, since that is when city hall, the federal courts and agencies, and other beats are fully functioning. On metropolitan dailies, the rewrite men are usually in a classification by themselves, of which more will be said later.

Rewrite is not the only device used by city editors to take up a general assignment reporter's spare time, however. Obituaries and funeral notices are done by reporters on papers too small to have an obituary editor, meaning most of them. It is a job never spoken of with enthusiasm by those who have to do it. Funeral notices are called in by the undertaker or by the family of the deceased. Material for an obituary is sometimes sent in by a family, or it may require a telephone call to them from a reporter—not the easiest kind of call to make, although there always seems to be someone not overcome by grief who is ready and willing to provide the needed information.

For public figures whose names make news even in death, newspapers carry proof sheets or typed background information sheets on numbers of people, the exact number depending on the size of the paper. Sometimes there are files of clippings concerning the deceased when he was still alive. All this material is kept in the paper's archives, which are known in this country as "the morgue," appropriate enough for obituary writing, but actually intended to cover a newspaper's entire file of clippings and photographs. These are used as background material for any kind of story.

Obituary material, when it is written ahead of time, has to be updated regularly. When a famous person is reported seriously ill, you can be sure that all over the country, editors will be instructing reporters, rewrite men, or obituary editors to see that the paper's filed obituary is up-to-date, and if not, to make it so. When the person dies, the story begins with that news as it came over the wire, and then follows immediately with the morgue obituary.

Obviously, the general assignment reporter's lot is not a continuous dash from the scene of one news event to another. The exciting news event is not necessarily an everyday occurrence, and in many of the smaller cities may not even be a weekly one. The reporter may be doing rewrite, taking death notices, writing obituaries, or just waiting. The assignments themselves may often be on the dull side. Covering the meetings of local organizations is not usually inspiring, and the general level of public speeches heard in small cities is seldom that of great oratory.

There are many other jobs besides general assignment reporting on the small city daily, and since the basic structure of such a paper is the general framework for all dailies, large and small, this may be the best place to describe them, with the variations occurring on metropolitan dailies left for a later chapter.

CITY EDITORS

Newsroom organization begins with the core operation centered in the city editor's desk. City editors, a legendary breed in themselves, are in direct charge of the news organization which covers the city news, from the reporters to the rewrite men, if any, and including the photographers. The city editor may have additional responsibilities, and, in any case, will probably need one or two assistants. His job is to direct the work of the reporters and photographers and to see that they meet the paper's deadlines.

COPY EDITORS

When he has okayed a story given to him by a reporter, it goes to the copydesk, traditionally in America a horseshoe-shaped affair presided over by the chief copyeditor who sits at a desk on the open head of the horseshoe; he is said to be sitting "in the slot." The copyeditors, ranged around the perimeter of the horseshoe, are said to be "on the rim." It is the job of the slot man, as the chief copyeditor is commonly called, to route the copy he gets from the city editor, from the telegraph editor handling domestic news (if there is one), and the cable editor (again, if there is one), and route all copy to the copyeditors on the rim. The rim man's job is to correct spelling and punctuation, if required; improve the language, if necessary; style it for the printer, as far as capital letters, paragraphing, and so forth are needed; and finally, to write a headline for it in a style dictated to him by the slot man.

All the copy (meaning stories) going into the paper must be routed through the copydesk in the city room, except the work of the sports department, which in most cases is autonomous and has its own copydesk. That department may not even be in the city room itself, but elsewhere in the building. City room copy comes from the city desk, the telegraph and cable desks, as noted, and also from the writers covering specialties like theatre and movies, real estate, special features, and other departments. On smaller papers, a single person may perform one or several of these jobs, not all of which exist on the smallest dailies. On the larger papers, they may be separate departments. This applies also to financial news, which may be the work of a single editor laboring alone, or of a department big enough to employ several people.

EDITORIAL DIRECTION

The overall direction of the editorial department is the responsibility of several executives, including the city editor and all assistants; the telegraph and cable editors, if there are any; the news editor; and the managing editor. Not all these smaller dailies have news editors, but if they do, they usually sit near the slot men and are the liaison between all the workers in the city room and the copydesk. The news editor controls the flow of news to the copydesk, sometimes eliminating a story he doesn't feel is sufficiently important, or requesting changes in it from the reporter or specialist who wrote it. In collaboration with the slot man, he decides on the relative importance of each story, determining its position in the paper and the prominence of the headline to be written for it.

Over all these executives is the magisterial figure of the managing editor, who does not usually sit in the city room with the others, but often in an adjacent office which has easy access in and out. He is the person who has overall responsibility for each day's editions, making decisions on whether or not to print a controversial story, directing the coverage of important stories, deciding matters of policy (if a question raised needs to go no higher) and in general, supervising the work of everyone else. The hand of a really good managing editor is felt in every department. In addition, he serves as the liaison between the city room and its executives, and the top echelon, which would include the editor (not often called these days by his old title, the editor-in-chief) and the publisher. Both these people are responsible to the paper's board of directors.

The editor presides over the editorial board and over the news conference, if the paper is large enough to have one. Both these terms require some explanation for the beginner. The editorial board consists of the editorial writers, who occupy their own quarters in the building, usually on another floor remote from the hustle and bustle of the city room where presumably they can think clearly. On small dailies, this work may be done by the editor and one or two assistants. On larger papers, the editor may simply direct a board of as many as a half-dozen or so editorial writers and do no writing himself. In that case, the editor's major job, besides conferring with the publisher and the managing editor on policy matters, is essentially a public relations one, aside from whatever role he may take in the day-to-day direction of the paper. That is, he represents the paper as a speechmaker at various events, attends conventions of his counterparts, and may even be involved with the business affairs of the company, with which the publisher is chiefly concerned.

The news conference is another matter. On papers large enough to have them, the editor sits down with the managing editor, the city editor, news editor, picture editor, telegraph and cable editors, and the make-up editor to discuss what's going into that day's edition of the paper. On the largest papers, even more executives may attend. On smaller ones, only three or four key people will be represented, if a news conference is held at all.

At these sessions, the news budget for the day is presented—local, state, national, and foreign—and if questions are raised about any story, they will be discussed. Each man or woman present tells what he has available, so that everyone gets a sense of what the news is for that edition and the relative importance of the stories. Obviously, if a big local story is breaking, it will get front page coverage with a large space allotment, consequently reducing available space for state, national, and foreign news. The amount of space available after the advertising has been placed is called the "news hole," and it is this space that is being generally allocated at the conference, although the exact measurements will later be the responsibility of the news editor, working with the make-up editor.

* * * * * *

Life on a small city daily is substantially what it is on a metropolitan daily, in miniature, with the exception that the work is likely to be less specialized and that quite often there is an overlapping of jobs.

Yet even the smallest small city dailies make ideal training grounds for people who want to work on big-time metropolitan dailies, since the work is so similar. But like the small town papers, they also provide a sense of identification and job satisfaction which thousands of newspaper people prefer to the greater specialization and relative anonymity of a large metropolitan staff.

CHAPTER 6

LIFE ON THE
BIG CITY NEWSPAPERS

It's always been hard to explain life on metropolitan dailies to people whose only source of information about them has been motion pictures, the theater, and perhaps a few books. Until *All The President's Men* was made, generations of Americans formed their impression of big city newspaper life from that perennial play and motion picture, *The Front Page,* and its many imitators.

The image presented by these productions was a city room bordering on chaos, with city editors yelling "Copy, boy!" at the top of their lungs and thrusting their tough jaws at cocky young reporters, saying, "Now go out and get that story and don't come back here without it." The city editor was customarily depicted as a tough/tender tyrant devoting all his time to breaking up sinister combinations of gangsters and politicians, while his reporters were shown to us as brash, fast-talking young men who spent their days tracking down criminals and breaking up gangs when they weren't drinking themselves to death.

All of these images had their roots in reality. There have been city editors, thankfully only a small minority, who were maniacs of one kind or another. They were epitomized in Charles Chapin, city editor of the old New York *World,* who took a ghoulish delight in disasters of all kinds. He is reputed to have told a reporter who had been thrown out of the office of one of the paper's enemies, "Go back there and tell that [expletive deleted] he can't intimidate me!" Chapin eventually murdered his wife and died in Sing Sing Prison. There were other city editors, notably on the Hearst papers of the 1920s, who thought of themselves as latter-day Chapins and made life miserable for their staff people.

But the image of the shouting, tyrannical city editor was usually a false one, and few of them ever uttered that classic line, "Stop the presses!" There *were* police beat reporters and city editors like those depicted in *The Front Page,* but again they were in the minority and are virtually non-existent today.

No more accurate depiction of life on a large metropolitan daily was ever given the public than in *All The President's Men,* with the obvious exception that investigative teams like Robert Redford and Dustin Hoffman exposing such historic scandals as the Watergate affair are not everyday occurrences. But the atmosphere of the city room itself, faithfully copied from the Washington *Post,* was accurate to the last detail, and it made everyone who saw it who had ever worked on a big paper feel that he was watching the story of his life. The actors who played newspaper editorial executives were light years away from *The Front Page* and its successors and were completely believable.

Somehow, the feeling for life on a big daily has completely escaped fiction writers, quite possibly because it doesn't have inherently dramatic qualities. Most of the drama in putting out a major daily, with infrequent exceptions, occurs outside the city room. Only two novels, both old ones, have captured what it is like to work on such a paper. One is *"The Great American Novel"* by Clyde Brion Davis (the title quotes are Mr. Davis'), and the other is *Splendor,* by Ben Ames Williams, both about newspapers of an earlier day.

Fed inadequately and inaccurately by books and movies, it is no wonder that the general public has little conception of how news is gathered and edited by that complex machine, the metropolitan daily. People have strange ideas about it. Those who hate the newspapers for one reason or another, and there are many of them, often believe that reporters roam the streets for news, completely overlooking worthy stories, intent only on dredging up scandal and corruption. Newspaper offices are commonly seen as places where villainous editors and publishers sit like spiders, concocting schemes to bring down politicians of the Other Party or planning ways to advance their own political ends.

In reality, as we've seen in talking about the small daily, newspapers are simply organizations devised to gather the news of what is happening in the community, state, nation, and world. Editors and publishers certainly have political views, which they advance legitimately in the editorial columns, but their chief concerns are to keep the paper viable economically and to get all the news they can, whatever it may be, without fear or favor. The reporters, as we've seen, don't wander aimlessly about looking for news, but are sent to where it is happening, has just happened, or may happen.

The framework in which all this takes place has been described in the preceding chapter, but the metropolitan daily has its own distinctive characteristics within that general pattern. The ultimate organization is that of the New York *Times,* but there is no point in employing it as a model, admirable though it may be, because it is unique. No other paper has a city room so large that its 140 or so reporters have to be summoned to the city desk for instructions by a public address system. No other paper has a staff so specialized that its reporters work almost entirely in their own fields.

On the mythically average big city daily, the focus of the paper is largely on local affairs, unlike the *Times,* whose tone is international, and which likes to call itself a paper of record, meaning that it is more inclusive than any other paper. The Washington *Post* concentrates on local affairs too, but since the locale is Washington, national affairs receive more coverage. Most metropolitan papers, while they cover national and foreign news to varying extents, are more interested in city hall and police headquarters. Since space for news is always limited, the inclination is to condense world and national news as much as possible, except for presidential happenings and congressional doings with local implications.

BEAT REPORTERS

The average metropolitan daily's city staff is the vital center of the paper, and covering the city hall and police beats may well be the most interesting part of it. These reporters become specialists if they stay on the beat long enough, and some are so happy doing this kind of work that they are unhappy if they are promoted to a city room job. On one midwestern paper, a police beat reporter who had given twenty devoted years to his job was supposedly rewarded by being brought into the city room and given a rewrite job at higher pay. Within a week, he was back at police headquarters. One of his problems was that he had telephoned in his stories for so many years that he no longer had the skill to write one quickly himself; another difficulty was that he sorely missed the familiar life of the beat.

This will not seem comprehensible to many beginners who find themselves assigned to that beat on their first job—as so many are, since it is traditional to break in new reporters there on all but the largest papers. (Many dailies have a policy of circulating new reporters around on all the beats at the beginning to see if they have any special talents and to give them a feel of the paper's whole news operation.) But to a young reporter covering his first metropolitan police beat, it may seem that he has been sent to Siberia. Press rooms in police headquarters are notoriously and historically places where anyone who was not being paid for it would not want to spend any time. Small, usually dirty, devoid of human comforts, the beats can also be lonely places in towns with only one newspaper.

The job itself is not a complicated one. It consists primarily of keeping track of what the department is doing at any given moment, through whatever system of reports it uses. When something occurs that is major enough, and continuing, so that a reporter can cover it, the beat man telephones his city room and a reporter is dispatched. Otherwise, the person on the beat spends most of his time looking for newsworthy items on the police blotter. On occasion he may have to interview a police official or a patrolman involved in an incident, and sometimes even a prisoner. If a municipal hospital is a part of the police headquarters complex, as it is in some cities, he will have to check from time to time with the emergency room to see if anything unusual is occurring. He may also have a list of telephone numbers of suburban police precincts not covered by stringers which he will call from time to time during the day or night period when he is on duty.

Successful police reporters are those who enjoy spending much of their time with policemen, who identify with their life, and share it vicariously. For such people, it can be a way of life, but for others, the police beat is only a way station on a reporter's progress upward, and on this beat everything else seems upward. It is about as far removed from the images projected by television's cops-and-robbers programs as it is possible to imagine.

The city hall press room usually is just as depressing physically, but at least the substance of the news there is more interesting. While the news itself may not be terribly exciting, it *is* undeniably the pulsebeat of the city's political life, and what goes on there affects all citizens. There is a great deal of news to be covered on the city hall beat, what with the mayor's office, the city council or aldermen, and the various city agencies; consequently, in larger cities two or three reporters may be required.

The danger in city hall reporting is that some beat men like the political life so well that they make a career of it and wind up being indistinguishable from the politicians. This is not good for them or the newspaper. But reporters who might have been politicians themselves (and quite a few go on to be just that) find this beat eminently satisfying.

One other beat of major consequence is the federal beat, which means the federal agencies, including the FBI, and the federal courts. In the largest cities, the courts themselves constitute a separate beat. Here, larger affairs are taking place than in city hall, but, on the whole, they are inclined to be duller. Many of the stories are highly complicated, and reporters with good qualifications are needed on this beat; those who did well in political and social science in college will find themselves right at home.

Court reporting is a specialty on many metropolitan papers. This involves the city court system, and perhaps the state courts if they happen to convene there. While there is far less drama in real life courtrooms than on television, there are enough newsworthy cases to make this kind of work interesting to reporters who find a perennial fascination in the workings of the law and see every trial as a small drama in itself.

BUREAU REPORTERS

In addition to beat work on newspapers, there are also the bureaus, wherever they may be. At the bottom of the pecking order are the bureaus which may be maintained in other cities of a state. One is certain to be in the state capital, if that is not in a major city, and there the job is legislative and court reporting. Or there may be special situations like that of the Providence, Rhode Island, *Journal-Bulletin,* which maintains bureau offices in the other newsworthy towns of that small state. New reporters are often assigned first to one of these bureaus for the "breaking in" process.

State bureaus are linked to the newspaper through the state desk in the city room, where the state editor handles not only the copy from the bureaus but also what is mailed or telephoned in by stringers. No matter in what part of this system a reporter labors, it is parochial work, like being on a small-town paper, and it is usually considered a step to better things.

OTHER SPECIALTIES

What are the better things? That depends on the interests of the reporter, but generally speaking, the opportunity to work exclusively in a field that he finds constantly absorbing and exciting is a better thing. Labor reporting, for example, can be a rewarding field these days, and these specialists will never be able to complain of having nothing to do. Some reporters find that their particular special talent is feature writing, and they wind up covering the news of the city that was once called "human interest"—that is, stories involving the daily life of humanity that isn't spot news. Feature writers usually are experts in interviewing, and they get assignments to interview visiting celebrities of every kind. Reporters who do this kind of work are often the incipient book and magazine writers on the staff.

The other daily specialties on the paper, as distinct from Sunday staff, would include sports, often an almost autonomous department; the arts, to which few metropolitan dailies devote much daily space except for motion pictures; and what used to be known as the women's pages, which today are more likely to be called by some euphemistic title like "Family Living."

We should not forget financial and business news, an important part of the metropolitan daily, although in some it is given only limited space. Newspapers have been slow to appreciate the importance of business news—of economic news in general—and their efforts to cover it have not always been outstandingly successful. But the overriding importance of world and domestic economic conditions in the last decade or so has caused many newspapers to upgrade this part of the paper and to look more seriously for knowledgeable people to write and edit the news in that department. That is good news for the business community generally, which has been complaining with justice for some time about inadequate and inaccurate coverage of its activities. Young reporters with an interest in these matters will find themselves much more in demand than those whose interests are more general, and they will discover a good many absorbing things to occupy their writing time.

The metropolitan daily is a collection of specialists, as you can see, with little general assignment work except on the smaller papers. Even then, reporters who do well covering one kind of story tend to be assigned to anything breaking in that field. In career terms, work on a big city daily offers the ultimate in money and prestige for the newspaperman. Remember, however, that it is a way of life that demands dedication, that tends to absorb people, and leaves them many times with limited time and energy for their life outside the paper. It is no accident that the divorce rate among people on metropolitan newspapers is well above average. At the same time, as on any paper, such work offers a front row seat for current events, and for many young newspapermen, there is no acceptable substitute.

CHAPTER 7

WORKING FOR THE WIRE SERVICES

Wire service work, as noted earlier, is often the first newspaper work a reporter does when he is breaking in as a stringer. The stringer system is the backbone of the wire services, which constitute a cooperative newsgathering organization that covers the globe and makes possible the volume of news that daily newspapers carry. In effect, it brings the world into the city room. Without these services, the range of a paper's news reporting would not extend beyond what its own staff could gather.

Oldest of the two major American wire services is the Associated Press (AP), dating to 1848 in its embryonic form, existing as Eastern and Western divisions during the latter part of the nineteenth century, and emerging in this century as a worldwide cooperative enterprise. The structure of the AP is like that of a club. A newspaper has to be elected to membership by the other memberships and is granted a franchise. Since there are restrictions which somewhat guarantee the value of the franchise, it has a definite value as a tangible asset and can be sold like any piece of real property, although only with the approval of the AP membership.

The United Press International, on the other hand, is simply a service that is for sale to anyone who can pay the price. It was begun in 1907 by E. W. Scripps, who founded the Scripps-Howard newspapers. Scripps, whose ideas at the time were more Populist than those of his fellow publishers, disliked the exclusivity of the AP franchise system. Believing that any publisher who wanted one should have his own wire service, he began what was to become the United Press. Two years later, in 1909, William Randolph Hearst inaugurated his International News Service (INS), an outgrowth of the leased wire services which already linked his newspaper chain. After a sometimes gaudy career, during which it distinguished itself largely in its foreign correspondence, INS was merged with the United Press in 1958, as part of the reorganization of Hearst's declining empire, to form United Press International (UPI).

In spite of their differences in organization, both these services operate in the same basic way. Stringers are the core, covering a single city or town, a county, several counties, or even a region within a state. Their work pours into the nearest city bureau, and the wire services have bureaus in every major American city, besides all the world capitals and other major foreign cities. The newspapers that are served by AP and UPI also contribute the news they gather, creating a vast interchange in itself.

Both agencies have their headquarters in New York City, the AP in its own building in Rockefeller Center, the UPI on several floors of the *Daily News* building on East 42nd Street. News flows in from the world to these headquarters and goes out again on several different systems to members and clients. Both agencies also have picture and feature divisions which distribute everything from news photos to comic strips. UPI, for example, through its subsidiary called United Features, harbors a small industry by itself through distribution of "Peanuts," the world's most popular comic strip.

The agencies also have large Washington staffs covering the White House and Capitol Hill, including political columnists whose work goes out on the wire too, serving especially the papers which do not have a Washington staff of their own. To compete with them, the New York *Times,* Washington *Post*, and Los Angeles *Times* syndicate the work of their Washington

Wire service bureaus make a tremendous volume of worldwide news available to daily newspapers.

writers. Still other columnists are available to newspapers through independent syndicates.

Both the AP and UPI have individual characteristics, giants though they are. The AP has historically based its reputation on the integrity of its report, and accuracy has always been its watchword, along with unbiased coverage of the news. The AP leans over backward so far to be unbiased that the traditional complaint among those who have worked for it is that it's worthy but dull. For many years, little latitude was given to AP reporters; what was expected of them was straight, factual, accurate reporting without any adornment. More freedom has been given in later years, but the tone of the AP is still conservative.

On the other hand, the UPI from the beginning had something of the pungent flavor of Scripps' personality, to which was added the flamboyance of his successor, Roy Howard. The UP was known for its bright, lively, feature quality and its willingness to be unorthodox, a willingness which on occasion got it into trouble. Merging it with International News Service meant that it was acquiring an organization not noted for its accuracy or lack of bias, but which was even livelier than the UP in its style. The INS personality has been pretty well submerged since it became the "I" at the end of the UP's logo.

All three of the services have been most celebrated, perhaps, for their foreign correspondence. In World War II, the names of such correspondents as Hal Boyle, Larry Allen, Daniel De Luce, all of the AP, became household words; all were Pulitzer Prize winners. An AP photographer, Joe Rosenthal, became famous for his picture of the Marines raising the flag on Mount Suribachi on Iwo Jima. Wes Gallagher and Don Whitehead were among its other noted reporters, covering both that war and the Korean conflict. In Vietnam, it was another AP photographer, Edward T. Adams, who snapped the picture of Saigon's police chief executing a Viet Cong prisoner on the street.

Ernie Pyle was a correspondent of the Scripps-Howard papers whose work, distributed by the UP, made him one of the best known reporters of our time. Among the UP war correspondents were such names as Webb Miller, Edward W. Beattie, Eleanor Packard, and Frank Tremaine. The INS, building on an earlier tradition that had begun with Floyd Gibbons and H. R. Knickerbocker, had people like James Kilgallen and Richard Tregaskis in the field. The service was particularly noted for its women correspondents, Inez Robb, Lee Carson, Dixie Tighe, and Rita Hume.

These are only a few of the wartime names, supplemented by others equally noteworthy in peacetime, that have become well-known to Americans in this century because their work was distributed through the wire services to nearly all the dailies in the country. That is one of the attractions of wire service work for a young reporter. If he eventually gets a job in the service, abroad or in Washington, or perhaps in the feature division, where his bylined work goes out on the wires, his name will become known to millions of people—or at least to those who are aware of the name that appears at the head of the stories they read.

Such fame, of course, is not the lot of most wire service people, who are often among the most anonymous of newspaper workers. Unless the circumstances are exceptional, a stringer cannot hope to get a byline. The next level is to work in a bureau, where the chances are only a little better; although if the bureau is in a large city the chances do improve. The UPI is traditionally more generous with bylines. Paying lower salaries than the AP before American Newspaper Guild contracts began to even things up, it was often said that the UP, and later UPI, paid off its people in bylines rather than dollars.

The aim of many reporters who intend to stay in wire service work, and who are laboring away in bureaus across the country, is to be transferred to New York, not only because it is at the center of operations but because it is the jumping off point to assignment in Washington or in one of the foreign bureaus. Needless to say, these assignments are coveted by a good many people and not everyone who aspires to get one succeeds. But the wire services do encourage young talent, and those who do good work can hope for one of these prize assignments, if that is their goal.

Otherwise, work in a bureau is much like working on a newspaper, except that the staff is small and general assignments are the rule. The specialists are mostly in New York. Bureau reporters cover local stories of sufficient general interest to go out on the wire. They also rewrite stories that appear in the local paper, or papers, which have the same general interest. There is nothing clandestine about this, of course. If a bureau isn't large enough to have its own quarters, it will probably be housed in or near the city room of a member or client newspaper, and the interchange is made freely since the newsgathering is cooperative. The AP and UPI are in competition with each other, not with the papers they serve.

Perhaps even more than regular reporters, wire service women and men must write rapidly and against constant deadlines. Economic conditions have reduced the number of editions on most newspapers to one or two, which makes the deadline situation much easier than it was in earlier days. It is the job of the wire service reporter, however, to get a breaking story on the wire just as soon as possible; consequently, his day can become a succession of deadlines. A breaking story will begin with a flash, two or three words, followed by a bulletin, a paragraph or so, succeeded by the story itself. Stories are received in newspaper offices on teleprinters, whose familiar chatter can be heard in every city room. Important stories involving flashes or bulletins are preceded by a bell signal on the machine, the number of bell strokes denoting the importance of the story.

In the average city bureau, there are not many stories in a week's work which merit ringing bells. The flow of news is no different than on a local paper, except that the bureau, as noted, covers only those items of general interest outside the city itself. Consequently, the number of stories it has to cover will always be much fewer than the number dealt with by the local paper's city staff. However, since there are also so few people to do the job, a bureau reporter may be on the street more than his local newspaper colleague. The bureau chief may also do some reporting on occasion, but his job is to direct the bureau's coverage, as the city editor does. His task is compounded by the fact that he must not only supervise the work of his reporters but also handle copy from stringers as it is telephoned or telegraphed in.

It is the bureau chief's job to see that the city, state, or region that he is responsible for is covered thoroughly and the stories put on the wire to New York as rapidly as possible. He is also on the receiving end of inquiries from New York, which may originate from the editors there or may be a query emanating from a member or client. The queries ask for more information on a story already transmitted or request the bureau to check on a report involving a particular area. The bureau chief's job is a busy one which may be a stepping stone for advancement within the organization or to executive jobs on newspapers.

Young reporters who go to work for wire services may get to see something of the country, since transfers from one bureau to another occur frequently. There is more mobility in this part of the newspaper business than in any other, which may be the primary reason young recruits stay in it and grow up within the organization. For those who have their eye on foreign correspondence, no other part of the business offers so many opportunities, difficult though these jobs may be to obtain. Few newspapers have foreign staffs any more, and since most have to rely on the wire services, there is little reduction in foreign coverage by the AP and UPI except for economic reasons.

The foreign bureaus operate in the same way as the domestic ones, covering the news of a capital city in the usual way and maintaining a system of stringers in other parts of the country. When major events occur requiring more help, reporters are assigned from other bureaus, either those nearby or from the well staffed offices in London and Paris, where foreign operations are centered.

Transmission of news to the United States is done by cable and radiotelephone. Satellite transmission has been a major help in speeding up coverage, but the bulk of news still moves by cable, in that esoteric language known as *cablese* which foreign reporters must learn. Cablese is based on the elimination of articles and prepositions and the combining of words, all done for the purpose of saving money on cable costs.

Between them, the AP and the UPI do an excellent job of covering the news of the world; however, since it is not humanly possible for the wire services to be everywhere, major newspapers often buy the services of national wire organizations in other countries. Oldest and best known of these is Reuters, the British service, which began in 1851 and employed pigeons to carry messages before wires came into general use. Reuters is also a worldwide organization, based in London, with offices in major American cities and serving more than forty papers here. Another important foreign service is Agence France-Presse, the French service which was particularly useful to American papers during the Vietnamese conflict because its correspondents were able to report from places like Hanoi where few American correspondents could penetrate. Agence France-Presse has been similarly useful in Asia and Africa at various times.

Some newspapers maintain foreign staffs today, but the great days of the New York *Herald Tribune* and Chicago *Daily News* correspondents have long since gone. Today the New York *Times,* Los Angeles *Times,* and Washington *Post* are the leaders, although the Chicago *Daily News, Christian Science Monitor* (especially noted for its coverage), and Baltimore *Sun* also have foreign bureaus in the important capitals. A few have at least a European bureau, with perhaps a few floating correspondents elsewhere, notably the Chicago *Tribune,* Minneapolis *Tribune,* Cleveland *Plain Dealer,* Toledo *Blade,* New York *Daily News,* San Francisco *Chronicle,* Washington *Star, Wall Street Journal,* and the Hearst newspapers.

To these must be added the worldwide correspondents' staffs of *Time, Newsweek, U.S. News & World Report,* McGraw-Hill *World News* and Fairchild Publications. As this television generation well knows, the three major networks also have bureaus in major capitals around the world. Operating out of these are roving correspondents who are ready to be moved to wherever news is breaking.

Foreign correspondence, since the days when James Gordon Bennett, Jr. sent Aloysius MacGahan to cover the wars of the Middle East and Asia in the latter part of the nineteenth century, has always been the most glamorous aspect of newspaper work. Some correspondents, like Richard Harding Davis, became national heroes during the Spanish-American War, and afterward, their books were widely circulated and their lives romanticized in magazines and other media. After Davis came such internationally known correspondents as Vincent Sheehan, Walter Duranty, Webb Miller, Leland Stowe, Marguerite Higgins, Homer Bigart, and other stars made by the wars they covered. Today's notables, unfortunately less well known, include people like Flora Lewis, the New York *Times'* European correspondent, whose reports on that continent's economic and social problems provide American newspaper readers with an informed, analytical view of events in Europe.

Wars breed big-name foreign correspondents (the Vietnamese conflict produced David Halberstam, among others), but the work of those who serve in peacetime is no less important, although it may not be as widely read. Working abroad, whether for the wire services or for one of the other organizations mentioned, is still an exciting, rewarding occupation.

For young reporters who go to work for wire services and find that they have a taste for political writing, the large Washington staffs of the AP and UPI offer opportunities. Of all the news bureaus in Washington, those of the wire services are the largest. The AP has more than a hundred people in Washington and the UPI more than eighty, both far outnumbering the New York *Times'* forty-two. (Reuters has more than twenty-two people in Washington.)

Viewed as a way of working life, wire services offer those entering journalism careers valuable experience in covering all kinds of news against constant time pressures, with, in the opinion of many, higher overall standards of accuracy than most newspapers maintain. Against the anonymity of the work, at least until a reporter rises to the New York, Washington, or foreign levels, must be balanced the mobility inherent in wire service organizations.

Not every wire service reporter, of course, gets to travel around the world, or even beyond the bureau in which he works. In that case, the young reporter will have to decide whether he likes this kind of work so well that he will stay with it and take his chances, or whether he will look for a job elsewhere in which he can use the experience he has gained.

CHAPTER 8

SUNDAY AND "WEEKEND" EDITIONS

The Sunday newspaper in America is not what it used to be, but then, as Dizzy Dean once observed, what is? Rising production costs have decreased the number of Sunday papers now published, and the competition of television and magazines has been felt in their advertising departments. Nevertheless, the Sunday newspaper, originated in the late nineteenth century by Joseph Pulitzer, continues to thrive in some cities. Even in such a leisure-oriented society as ours, where a dozen other things compete for attention on Sunday, the newspaper offers familiar relaxation before the day begins.

The comic section was for many years the chief selling point of the Sunday paper, an idea pioneered by Hearst; the Katzenjammer Kids (still appearing) was the first really popular strip. The color comic section which Hearst originated had become a staple feature of newspapers by the 1920s, sometimes running sixteen pages or more. It became one of the victims of television, though, and while it is far from dead, it no longer has the vitality it once had. A new generation wrapped up in television and the movies is not much amused. Still, they are a staple feature of nearly every Sunday paper.

For a long time, too, Sunday papers usually had a "roto section," meaning a picture section printed in brown ink by the rotogravure process. The arrival of picture magazines, and then of television, ended the career of the roto section, which in fact foreshadowed the magazines. Now *Life* and *Look,* the two great picture periodicals, are also dead.

Sunday magazines offer opportunities for food, travel, fashion, and other special-interest writers.

Newspapers found that one way they could compete with both magazines and television for advertising in their Sunday editions was to carry a magazine supplement. The idea caught on quickly, and the Sunday newspaper magazine has become an institution in itself, with several national publications in existence, distributed to newspapers all over the country. *This Week,* now defunct, was the first successful one, with *Parade* (still functioning) and others following. Some newspapers began their own Sunday magazine sections and did well with them. In order to meet competition, many newspapers have felt that they must carry every magazine available to them for Sunday distribution, along with the magazine-like advertising folders, so that the physical fallout from some papers when they're opened on Sunday morning is considerable—a half-dozen or so supplements of various kinds.

The two largest Sunday newspapers in the United States are the New York *Times* and the Los Angeles *Times.* Legendary tales are told about their bulk. For example, one of the pre-Christmas issues of the New York *Sunday Times,* when holiday merchandising brings advertising and the number of pages to their annual peak, was being flown to some remote place when a copy of the edition slipped from the plane and fell to earth, striking and killing a cow grazing in a lonely field—no doubt an apocryphal story. The Los Angeles paper, it is said, has such difficult suburban delivery problems with the huge Sunday edition that its delivery boys have to make two trips to their customers' doorsteps, bringing half the paper on the first trip and the other half later.

In keeping with its institutional character, the New York *Sunday Times* is as unique as the daily. It has never carried a Sunday comic section (nor does the daily have comics), and it has never carried a variety of magazine supplements, staying with the two of its own which have become institutions in their own right—the *Book Review* and the *Sunday Magazine.* Both are among the leading advertising media in America, and the *Book Review* is considered by most people in the publishing business as the foremost reviewing medium in the country. Its nearest rival is the Chicago *Tribune's* Sunday *Review of Books.*

The average Sunday paper in America has become a more or less standardized product, although there are variations. The size of each one, of course, is determined by the amount of advertising the paper is able to obtain, and that appears to be limited mostly by the economic health of the city and the nation; competition from one or more local sources may also cut it down.

Sunday staffs are recruited both from within and without the paper. It is common practice for those who work on the daily to write "Sunday pieces" in addition, usually for a little more in their paychecks. But on large metropolitan Sunday papers, the Sunday department is nearly autonomous, functioning as a paper within a paper. Nevertheless, its work has to be closely coordinated with the news department, particularly in the composing room and in the matter of deadlines. A Sunday editor directs the process, usually with the help of assistants, but otherwise the paper breaks down into sections, with an editor for each section. One copydesk serves everyone, in most cases, although a departmental editor is likely to do his own copyediting.

A Sunday newspaper most often begins with a colored comic section wrapped around the outside to give it visibility on the newsstand, even though that is no longer necessary in one-newspaper towns. Inside are the news sections, on Sunday carrying not only the spot news of that day but a variety of background and feature stories of a less timely nature. The comic section comes through a syndicate, and the news section is prepared in the news room (to use a term more common today than city room). Everything else is in the domain of the Sunday editor, except for whatever syndicated magazine supplements the paper may buy, and with one other exception—sports.

What the "everything else" encompasses depends on the kind of Sunday newspaper the management is trying to produce, but there are standard ingredients. One is a feature section, by whatever name it may be called, which will carry full-length local feature stories and probably movie and theater news and advertising as well. Many of these feature sections have been compressed into magazine-sized supplements, with the amusement coverage dropped into another section, or in some cases given its own section.

Another standard Sunday section is real estate, with few exceptions used chiefly as a promotion device for advertisers. This has been the case traditionally, but lately there have been papers which use this section to discuss urban problems, to talk about architecture, and to provide people with housing information. The New York *Times* is a model in this respect, although it is so heavy with advertising that little space remains for other articles.

Travel may well be a separate section, unless it is reduced to a few pages or columns in another section. Like real estate, it is most often used as a supplement to the advertising. Not many papers have the courage to say in their travel pages that travelers may have serious problems in one resort or another, or that certain advertised places ought to be avoided. In most of these sections, it is difficult to tell the advertising from the text matter, much of which may come from the advertisers and go into the paper virtually unedited.

Sunday papers devote a good deal of space to women's traditional interests, making few concessions to feminism. In the last quarter-century, food has come to dominate these pages, and Sunday papers are likely to devote considerable space to recipes, party planning, and consumer features in general. Many papers now have food editors who write columns for the daily paper and handle the Sunday food pages or section in the bargain.

There is so much variation in the way Sunday financial sections are prepared that it's hard to generalize about them. Sometimes they are entirely the product of the staff that produces the daily financial pages, but if the paper is large enough, it may have an entire Sunday financial staff. In any case, it's a good bet that the daily writers will also be appearing on Sunday. Sunday staff writers are likely to do mostly background and summary stories about the week's financial events. Although these pages may be heavy with financial advertising, besides various market summaries, there is seldom any collusion with advertisers as there is in real estate and travel.

A few papers imitate the New York *Times'* famed "News of the Week in Review" section. This Sunday feature carries the editorial and Op-Ed page seen every day and summarizes the news in short, signed background pieces broken down into categories. For many years, nothing was signed in this section except pieces by foreign and Washington correspondents; now bylines appear at the ends of stories. The idea of the section is not only to summarize the chief news events of the week in all the .major areas of human activity, but to give them some perspective by means of background, analysis, and, occasionally, forecast.

Imitators customarily make something of a grab bag out of this section, throwing into it editorials, political columns and background stories, analytical stories from the wires, and local political stories. However it is done, this section is likely to be the least read in the Sunday paper, with only two or three exceptions among the major metropolitan dailies—the result of poorly defined purpose and slipshod overall direction.

The sports section appears much as it would on any other day, but it may have more background pieces and may also include a page on boating, photography, or some other sports-related hobby. The problem with Sunday sports sections is that they usually close too early to get a great deal of the important spot news in, and so they must depend heavily on stories written before events and on background stories.

If the paper has a separate amusements section, the average effort in this direction is not much to inspire enthusiasm. Advertising will be heavy, and around it will appear a few local reviews of movie or theatre or music productions. There usually is also a great deal of material from public relations people and press agents which has been edited slightly. Some papers, however, do make a serious effort to cover the cultural life of the community with reviews, features, pictures, interviews, and background stories about events in that field. Done properly, these sections can be a great encouragement and help to local cultural organizations. Done poorly, as they so often are, they can be a press agent's junkpile.

Working on a Sunday paper means writing for one or more of these departments, plus editing copy in many cases. While reporting skills are paramount requirements on daily papers, writing and editing talents and expertise in one or several fields are more important on Sunday papers. Daily reporters who want

Covering music, drama, film, and other events, critics are important staff members on many daily newspapers.

to get into a specialized field find work on a Sunday section dealing specifically with that field to be a good point of entry. If the paper has a book review section, for instance, an inquiry to the literary editor may produce some reviewing assignments, which represent extra money and will possibly open the door to working on that section. The same thing can be said for other parts of the cultural vineyard covered by the paper. It is often not difficult to get into doing this kind of work yourself, as long as the editor-writer in the field doesn't think you're trying to get his job.

Travel editors, by the nature of their job, reap benefits beyond what any paper can do for them. They are invited to openings of new resorts, to inaugural flights of airlines and sailings of ships, to hotel openings, and on other kinds of junkets connected with the travel industry. While it is considered unethical to accept any kind of gift in return for a story, travel seems to be an exception because it is part of a travel editor's or writer's job to cover the kind of thing to which he is being invited. The conscientious editor or writer accepts the free trips and rooms and meals with the understanding that he will not necessarily write glowingly in praise of wherever he has been. In practice, however, as noted earlier, few critical words appear in most of these travel sections.

Beauty and fashion editors are subjected to the same kind of pressures, and their desks are often covered with new products which their makers hope will be written about favorably. They usually are, but probably because the editor-writer chooses the things which are likely to please and interest readers.

Motion picture publicity departments sometimes try to woo Sunday and daily critics and writers by various means, but they are a highly resistant lot—especially now, when movies are taken so much more seriously in print than they used to be.

In brief, working on a Sunday newspaper is considerably better for many journalists than the day-to-day grind of reporting, unless one is a specialist in an absorbing field. But that is what the Sunday paper offers, too—an opportunity to specialize. Certainly the working conditions are better: a regular work day, a good part of the weekends free, and no daily deadline pressures. However, those who imagine that having a weekly deadline is easier don't know the building-up process to that closing deadline, usually sometime Saturday. Sunday editors and writers have more time to do their jobs, but what they do inevitably *takes* more time.

Because it is a weekly operation and because it is divorced physically and in function from the news room, the atmosphere in the Sunday department of a newspaper is quite different, more like that of a magazine. People who have worked in both fields find them quite similar. The difference, however, is that magazine people are working with ideas directed to a specific audience which is well defined by market research, and everything is directed toward reaching that market. The Sunday newspaper, much as it may often resemble magazine content, is meant to appeal to a much broader readership and cannot afford to zero in on any single element of its readership. Since the appeal is broader, it is also more bland, and so writing and editing for Sunday papers is not as varied as magazine work, tending to be more a simple extension of the regular weekly paper.

In spite of these limitations, Sunday newspaper work is a satisfying occupation for those who would rather stay in the newspaper business than go to a magazine, and who are not addicted to the preoccupation with hard news that characterizes the news room.

WEEKEND EDITIONS

Some dailies try to take advantage of weekend advertising without going to the expense of a regular Sunday edition. The compromise is a so-called "weekend edition," which appears on Saturday morning (occasionally as late as the afternoon) and is intended to sell through the weekend, although most of the circulation is confined to Saturday.

The weekend edition is usually no more than a Saturday edition of the regular paper, considerably cut back in the news department, but often containing a large magazine insert. The insert has a variety of feature material, some produced by the paper's own staff but a great deal of it likely to be syndicated. Weekend television listings will probably be carried, perhaps with accompanying stories or boxes that summarize what is being offered in movies or sports. Amusements will be covered, bolstering the heavy advertising in that department. This may also be the only occasion on which books are reviewed, by papers that won't be bothered with it during the week. The reviews may be staff written or bought from a syndicate. An excellent book review column has been distributed by the AP for years and is used by many papers.

While the weekend edition is largely put out by the regular staff, it will probably have an editor or two in charge of it, offering further job opportunities closely related to Sunday department work. Most of these editors are likely to be working at other jobs on the paper as well.

CHAPTER 9

NON-EDITORIAL JOBS
ON NEWSPAPERS

To most people, a career in newspapering means writing and editing, and the word *newspaperman* quite often is equated with the word *reporter.* Editors and what they do are not clearly understood and the copyeditor's job is comprehended by few outside the business.

Beyond the news room, however, is a large domain which keeps the paper functioning as a business organization. No matter what a paper does in getting the news and displaying it, the viability of any newspaper is determined by the successful functioning of its business side. The editorial department can produce a good, bad, or indifferent paper, and the results may or may not influence the fate of the publication. A good many newspapers are less than mediocre products, measured by professional standards, but they survive because of their particular situations. If the paper's non-editorial organization fails to do its job properly, however, it will die.

These non-editorial jobs have their equivalents in the business world, since a newspaper is essentially a business, and people with an interest in business have to be recruited for them. Yet they are different, too, because newspapers are not like any other business enterprise, and the relationship between management and workers is not quite the same.

The non-editorial side of a newspaper includes the advertising and circulation departments, the legal department, the accounting department (which includes payroll), the promotion department, and the overall business management. We're talking here about metropolitan dailies; the organization is much simpler on a small paper, where the publisher and editor may handle all the business affairs of the publication with the help of an accountant and/or a bookkeeper.

To begin at the top, the publisher and his assistants, who may be vice-presidents or have other titles, take care of the physical and financial life of the paper. Their duties are many. A paper has constant dealings with its banks, particularly if it is one which has diversified and owns other properties. It is also deeply involved with real estate and the maintenance of it. Equipment must be purchased, and there is the constant struggle to get paper, ink, and other essential supplies. Unions must be dealt with, both on the editorial and mechanical sides, and negotiations may involve seven or eight different unions whose contracts expire at separate times.

The largest papers have executives who spend all or most of their time on labor matters, and their legal departments often are involved as well. A paper may hire a law firm on a retainer basis or may have a full-time legal staff. In special cases, as when a Constitutional matter has to be decided, an outside expert may be retained. The movie version of the newspaper lawyer has him spending his time and energies on libel actions, but in reality there are relatively few libel suits filed against newspapers. A newspaper's lawyer is much more likely to be working on union problems, or on the same kind of corporate law he would be practicing with any other large business.

As such an organization, the newspaper has the usual quota of business jobs available—that is, secretaries, accountants, clerks, operators of business machines, typists, and personnel people. Is there any difference, then, in working for a newspaper rather than for some other kind of business? As far as the actual work is concerned, the answer is no; job duties are substantially the same.

The differences are that, at a newspaper, you would be working in a smaller company than one of the big corporations, and that even though you might be remote from the scene of action, you would belong to a news organization.

ADVERTISING DEPARTMENT

In the advertising department, however, the situation is different. This department is three-sided—local display, national, and classified—each one doing a different kind of job. Let's look at the last first, because classified advertising is the bread-and-butter of a newspaper. Those long columns of fine print you see in the classified sections are the product of a hard-working group of people who not only process the ads that people want to place in the paper, but also solicit advertising which has to do with businesses and services. The soliciting is accomplished by telephone, as is much of the ad-taking. Newspapers usually have sub-stations in various parts of a large metropolitan area where people come to place classifieds. The ad-taker often must help the customer in phrasing the advertisement as briefly and clearly as possible.

You will note in the classified sections of your paper, especially on Sunday, that the ads are broken down into categories. There usually are two kinds of ads—the usual five or six lines of one type size, and the larger ads using varying type sizes, known as display classified. People who work in this field become expert in one or more categories, and display specialists understand how to get the most out of that kind of advertising.

Local display ads are the offerings of local merchants—department stores, clothing stores, amusements, specialty shops, and, in fact, the whole range of merchandising. The people in this department work closely with the merchants helping them write their ads or cooperating with the advertising department of a store. The position of the ad is an important element in this process, along with other considerations. Large newspapers have someone in the department who rules on acceptance, that is, whether a particular ad violates good taste or might offend readers in some other way. Sometimes this kind of censorship goes to ridiculous extremes, but often it protects readers from spurious schemes, fraudulent claims, and offerings harmful to the health. Newspapers are not required by law to print an advertisement that they deem unacceptable.

National advertising involves the solicitation of ads from merchandisers who have countrywide distribution, like automobile companies, firms that manufacture appliances, or food companies. The work in this part of the advertising department is basically the same as it is for magazine ad salespeople, or those who sell time on radio and television. Time is what electronic journalism and entertainment are selling; space is what newspapers and magazines are marketing; consequently, their sales force consists of *space salespeople*. The largest newspapers have national advertising offices in various major cities, but most use the services of what are known in the business as *ad reps* —advertising sales organizations which maintain offices in major cities and represent several newspapers.

Working in any division of a newspaper's advertising department requires the basic urge to be in this kind of business, whether newspaper or not, and a talent for selling, writing, or both. Billing and collection are part of the ad department's work, too, but this may be merely a subsidiary of the business department.

CIRCULATION DEPARTMENT

Circulation is an entirely different kind of occupation. It involves two things: getting the newspaper to its customers after it's printed, and dealing with the vendors who distribute it. The work of the circulation department begins when the folded papers roll off the presses into the mailing department, where they are wrapped in bundles, tied with wire, and loaded into the fleet of trucks waiting for them. Some of these trucks service the city's newsstands, which may be on street corners, in stores, at airports, bus and rail terminals, and in all kinds of retail establishments where newspapers are sold. Other bundles of papers go to distributors who service the paper's circulation zone; their customers are the local drugstores, hotels, and stores where newspapers are bought by the public.

Circulation is concerned, then, with the physical means of distribution, which means a fleet of trucks for the city and other vehicles to supply the out-of-town distributors. That puts the circulation department in the transportation business. Since all these dealers, except those who are the distributor's customers, are clients of the paper, there is a great deal of paperwork involved in dealing with them.

In the days when there was fierce competition among competing dailies for space on the newsstands, circulation departments were run by strong men who took strong actions. In the Chicago of the 1920s, for example, there were bloody circulation wars among the papers in that city. These usually involved organized crime figures and resulted in many deaths and injuries. In the late 1930s, when the experimental newspaper *PM* was scheduled to appear on the stands, the New York *Daily News,* employing some of the milder methods of the 1920s, tried to prevent its appearance. But that kind of competition has disappeared today, because no such competitive situation exists in any American city. Newspaper circulation departments today are run by business managers whose preoccupation is distribution by antiquated methods which may be overtaken in time by new technology.

To most people, a career in newspapering means writing and editing, but with development of photojournalism, the photographer has become an important member of the news team.

PROMOTION DEPARTMENT

The promotion department is an important element in the non-editorial side of a newspaper. A newspaper must promote itself to several audiences: to the public at large (its potential customers); to special audiences within that public; and to potential advertisers. The most visible evidence of its work is the kind of outdoor advertising of the paper which appears on its own delivery trucks. As newspaper vans move about the city, their sides usually are plastered with posters advertising some current feature in the newspaper—a column, a comic strip, an investigative report of some kind.

But that is only the beginning of the promotion department's work. Its posters, streamers, and other devices to publicize something in the paper can be seen on newsstands, billboards, and at the retail distribution points. Some papers—at least those able to afford it—are using television commercials to advertise their merits and get new readers. Radio commercials and sponsored programs have been in use for some time.

To reach special audiences, the promotion department organizes community contests of various kinds, or sponsors activities in a particular part of the city where it hopes to get increased circulation. All that is in addition to large citywide promotions, like the sponsoring of major athletic and other events. Two of the best examples are the Chicago *Tribune's* All-Star football game and in New York, the Harvest Moon Ball, a dance contest originated and sponsored by the *Daily News* for many years. The *Tribune's* promotion department, in fact, devised and carried out many community events to promote the interests of what the *Tribune* called "Chicagoland," which of course also promoted the paper's readership.

The promotion department uses leaflets, brochures, and other printed material to get the newspaper into the public consciousness. To cite the *Tribune* again, one of the most successful promotions it devised was a pamphlet called "Trees to Tribunes," which told in simple terms the story of how paper was produced from the trees cut on the paper's acreage in Quebec, and was then transported down through the Great Lakes to Chicago, where it was automatically transferred to the presses. Hundreds of thousands of copies were distributed.

The public gets much of this printed information as the result of plant tours, which are usually conducted by the promotion department. On the largest papers, like the New York *Times,* tours of the plant for visitors always have been regarded as an excellent promotional device. Since the troubled decade of the 1960s, however, many newspapers have either curtailed or eliminated their tours for security reasons.

As you can see, the promotion department does its work along a broad front, concerning itself with a great many activities. Working in such a department requires specialized talents and interests. Anyone considering promotional work would have to ask himself whether he would rather do it for a newspaper than elsewhere, because newspaper promotion work is basically the same as it is on magazines, broadcasting, book publishing, or in the larger field of product promotion. Those who have the talent and essential interest will choose newspapers if the particular problems and challenges of that medium appeal to them.

PHOTOGRAPHY DEPARTMENT

We come at last to that unrelated field, photography, which is closely allied with the editorial side, yet not concerned with writing and editing. News photography is a fascinating, often exciting profession which goes back to the Civil War, when photography itself was new. There were no news photographers as such in that war, but certainly many of the famed Mathew Brady's photographs were news photographs. One thinks especially of his picture of Lincoln making the historic Gettysburg Address.

News photography as an occupation came into being near the end of the nineteenth century. It was not the flexible, versatile kind of work it became later because the equipment then was large, heavy, and awkward. For a time, all interior shots had to be taken with the aid of flashpowder in a pan at the end of a long stick which someone, often the photographer himself, had to hold. The powder was ignited at the moment the picture was snapped, providing illumination for the primitive lens. Newspaper history is full of stories about unfortunate uses of flash powder—wedding parties transfixed into expressions of horror by the explosion, and a famous shot of a six-day bicycle race in the old Madison Square Garden, when an oversupply of powder in the pan created such a blast as the picture was taken at the start of the race that the bicyclists, when the smoke cleared away, were found distributed along the track in various states of shock and anger.

But then a famous instrument, the Speed Graphic, was invented, and news photographers carried it everywhere news was breaking, in war and in peace.

News photographs became an essential part of newspapers in the 1920s. Publishers who had been reluctant to do much with photography before were compelled to change their minds by the advent of the highly successful tabloids, whose stock in trade was pictures—the more sensational the better. People were attracted to the occupation for the same reason they came into reporting— the constant variety, the front-row seat, the meeting of all kinds of people in every conceivable kind of circumstance.

Today news photography is a wide-ranging field, producing, with sophisticated modern equipment, pictures which are not only newsworthy but artistic accomplishments as well. Some news photographers have gone on to become well known artists in their field. On many smaller papers, reporters have to take the pictures as well as write, and that ability is a hiring prerequisite. Larger papers have their own photography departments, with a director, technical facilities ranging all the way from adequate to elaborate, and a corps of highly skilled professionals who take the pictures. Often photographers and reporters work together as a team, going out on stories in a staff car. The common procedure on a breaking story is for the reporter, once he gets an assignment from the city desk, to go to the photography department, where a photographer is assigned to him.

News photographers not only take pictures of news while it is happening—such spot news as riots, picketing, sports, demonstrations, meetings of newsworthy people—but also those activities which convey the mood of a city at a particular time—the aftermath of a big storm or people on a quiet holiday or a particularly cold or hot day. The photographer's work can be utterly routine—meetings of officials, politicians shaking hands, or individuals being interviewed—or it can be exciting, even dangerous, if the photographer is present where events are taking place. Photographers have especially distinguished themselves taking pictures of wartime action, in which many have been killed.

The news photographer's job requires speed, ingenuity, persistence, and courage, besides the usual technical qualifications. News photographers have always been a breed apart, often brash and outspoken, feeling a sense of comradeship with each other, as though they belonged to an exclusive fraternity. Newspaper work is a particular kind of photography which appeals to a particular kind of photographer.

* * * * * * * *

As you can see in this chapter, putting out a newspaper requires a multitude of talents, not all of which are in the visible writing and editing which readers see. The other jobs are numerous and have their equivalents in other businesses, but they have a common basis in the living, vital organism which is a newspaper.

CHAPTER 10

PREPARING FOR A
NEWSPAPER CAREER

For those who plan a career in newspaper work, a major decision they must make is what kind of education to pursue. At some point on the road to making this decision, the student is almost certain to encounter the argument that on-the-job training is all he needs, that it's a mistake to consider a journalism school or department.

This argument comes not only from people in the profession (especially from those who still think it's a trade), but from academicians who regard journalism training as a vocational intrusion on the sanctity of liberal arts programs. It must be remembered that education in journalism has had to struggle against both these forces from the time the University of Missouri launched the first program in 1909. Joseph Pulitzer, in fact, had been trying to endow a journalism course at Columbia University since 1904, but Nicholas Murray Butler, then the president of the University, so hated everything Pulitzer represented that he refused to take the money. It was a year after Pulitzer died in 1911 before he consented to take the bequests in the publisher's will which established the School of Journalism (a graduate school since 1935) and the celebrated Pulitzer Prizes.

Other schools and departments sprang up across the country, and some established formidable reputations, but even the best had to combat opposition from liberal arts purists who wanted to abolish or curtail them, and from self-made editors, publishers,

and other newspapermen who felt themselves threatened by the advance of an educated elite. This opposition, from both sources, is beginning to crumble. The sharp increase of vocationalism in general and the dramatic upward surge of journalism education enrollments in the past ten years have combined to mute the academic attack, although the diehards persist. There are diehards in the newspaper business, too, but they are disappearing, simply because the schools and departments have now heavily populated the entire communications industry.

It is also important to remember, however, that formal journalism education is not essential to get a job in the business, nor to succeed in it. A great many writers and editors have had no such training, and it *is* possible to "learn on the job," provided someone will hire you and take the time to teach you. There are, too, individuals who have so much natural talent they seem to know instinctively what to do and how to do it.

Why study journalism then? There are several good reasons. One is that it will save you a substantial amount of career time. A graduate of a good journalism school or department will have such a comprehensive background in the basic skills and so much specialized knowledge to go with it, that he will be able to take a newsroom job the day after he graduates. Some diehards in the business still refuse to believe this fact, which is confirmed by the experience of thousands of graduates. Old guard newspapermen still insist that a journalism school graduate with a master's degree has to start as a copyboy and work up in the traditional way. This illogical and wasteful practice seems to be disappearing—and about time, because the newspaper business has lost a good many able young graduates who did not choose to put up with this old-fashioned nonsense and went into some other part of communications, or even chose some other vocation. If you go to a journalism school, then, don't let anyone in the profession denigrate your degree by virtue of his ignorance and prejudice. You are the only one who can lower its value, by not learning to do your job well.

Another reason for studying journalism is the opportunity it offers you to survey the career possibilities available in the whole area of communications. A good school or department will offer course sequences in newspaper work, magazine work, public relations, broadcast journalism, and in a few places, advertising as well. Many offer undergraduate and graduate programs in communications theory, "the sociology of journalism," which has now become a virtual necessity for teaching in the field.

To cite still another reason for journalism study, if the work is done with skilled professionals who are still at work themselves, which is the case in the best schools, it is equivalent to a year's training in a news room, and probably better, because it is training not acquired by chance or by making mistakes that can get you fired. The work and atmosphere of a news room is created, offering many opportunities to meet and talk with working professionals to learn what is going on in the business. There are other reasons for journalism study, but these three are sufficient in themselves.

The next question is, When should training begin? And the answer is, As soon as possible. Some students don't discover the attractions of journalism until they're in college, or about to enter, and there are many who switch into it as late as their junior year, after they have completed two years of work in some other field. In these cases, nothing is wasted. Let's say that a girl has embarked on a physical education curriculum, then decides it's some kind of journalism career that she's wanted all along. She will probably not realize that her physical education background has prepared her for jobs she may never have thought of. Combining that training with journalism may open the doors to well-paying jobs in the promotion departments of big sporting goods companies, or to the sports pages of newspapers. With this dual background, she will have multiple career choices.

People who are going to commit themselves to the newspaper business, however, usually discover while they are in high school that this is the only way of life for them. And these students are probably already doing something about it. They are gaining valuable experience by working on the high school paper and yearbook, and no doubt they are active in whatever literary work is available in the school. But students involved in such activities should be careful of one thing—they should not permit themselves to ignore subjects in which they are not particularly interested. Newspaper people, and in fact all writers, need to fill their minds with as much knowledge in as many fields as possible. Paraphrasing Rousseau, nothing human should be alien to them. Everything a writer learns is useful to him at some time, and a broad range of knowledge gives him perspective on human affairs.

SELECTING A SCHOOL

When it comes to selecting a journalism school or department, you may wish to consult the pamphlet, *Education for a*

Journalism Career, prepared by the American Council on Education for Journalism, an accrediting organization. It can be obtained free from Milton Gross, Secretary-Treasurer, ACEJ, School of Journalism, University of Missouri, Columbia, Missouri, 65201. This pamphlet lists the college and university journalism programs accredited by the organization. Programs accredited include news-editorial, advertising, broadcast news, radio-television, general, public relations, magazine, technical journalism, agriculture, photojournalism, publishing, and home economics.

For further information, especially in the area of financing your education, you may want to acquire a copy of the *Journalism Scholarship Guide and Directory of College Journalism Programs,* prepared by the Newspaper Fund, and obtainable free from The Newspaper Fund, Inc., P.O. Box 300, Princeton, New Jersey, 08540. This extremely valuable booklet lists, by states, the schools and departments of journalism offering scholarships; additionally, it gives information about the financial help offered by newspapers and professional societies, minority grants, and miscellaneous scholarships and internships. The booklet gives you correct names, telephone numbers, and zip codes of the universities and colleges; the name of the person heading it; a listing of sequences offered (accredited sequences are underlined); and a notation of degrees offered. Besides all this useful information, the Guide will give you a one-paragraph summary of average yearly school costs at each institution listed.

Armed with these guides, you, as a prospective journalism student, should first decide what area of the country you want to study in—a decision that will, no doubt, be influenced by family and financial factors. If you feel free to go anywhere, you will be free to choose from the best known programs in large schools, as well as from those offered in smaller institutions. In any case, you should zero in on three or four places which appeal most to you and where financial help is available if you need it. Give yourself some latitude, because there is always the possibility that you may not be accepted by your first choice, or even the second.

If it is at all possible, you should visit the institution itself, meet the dean or head if he is available, talk to professors and students, perhaps even ask to sit in on a class. There is no better way to get the "feel" of a school than by this process. By visualizing yourself in that setting, with these people, you can get at least some preliminary idea of whether you'll be happy there.

CURRICULUM

Once the choice is made and you've been accepted and enrolled, there are other things to remember as you begin your work. The most important, of course, is the curriculum. In all accredited institutions, and in many non-accredited ones, you will find that your professional training is limited to approximately one-fourth of your total credits. (At New York University, for example, you are permitted 32 credit hours in the Department of Journalism, out of 120 required for the degree.) While that rule may seem confining to some people, it makes sense. Being a journalist requires the broadest possible background knowledge, and without the rule there would be many students so carried away by the professional courses that they would take little else.

In institutions where "area" course requirements still prevail, you'll be required to take a diversity of subjects in different fields of knowledge. But in schools where such program requirements have been abolished, you will simply have to keep in mind that you need to know as much as possible about a lot of things; therefore, diversify your curriculum as much as you can outside the journalism courses. If your school permits program minors, try to specialize in a department related to your long-range goals. People who want to be political writers, for example, need to take as much political science and history as they can. Science writers, obviously, need a science background.

The journalism school or department itself will require some basic courses, and these should be taken as soon as possible. During your freshman and sophomore years, you should be thinking about the area of communications in which you want to specialize, and the last two years will be spent largely in taking those specialized courses.

GRADUATE SCHOOL

After graduation you must make another decision: Should I go right to work or enter graduate school? Often, financial conditions will make that decision for you, without argument. But if graduate school is possible, the question is whether to go for a master's or a doctorate degree and whether it should be in a graduate journalism program or elsewhere. All these questions really ought to be decided on an individual basis, but some general observations can be made.

For people who feel confident of the professional preparation they got in their undergraduate training, and who have decided to go into a part of the communications business that requires a good deal of background, it may be wise to get a graduate degree in some field other than journalism. Political science, history, one of the sciences, even the law are all possibilities; others depend on particular interests and ambitions. If you choose the kind of specialization that graduate programs in journalism offer, a glance at the guides mentioned earlier in this chapter will disclose that the accredited programs are at Columbia, Northwestern, California (Berkeley), American University, and the University of Michigan. While these are excellent programs, there are others of high quality which are not accredited and ought to be investigated, among them, those at the University of Missouri, Southern

California, Illinois, Minnesota, and Wisconsin. Others, like those at Syracuse and Boston University, offer specialties of their own. Look over the field, then, and see which one best fits your needs.

Graduate programs are not easy to get into because their popularity has been growing significantly, and all limit the number of students they admit. At the prestigious Graduate School of Journalism, Columbia University, for example, a thousand or so persons apply and between 125 and 150 are accepted.

The primary difference among the graduate schools is the varying emphasis they place on specialized professional training beyond the undergraduate level, as opposed to communications research, which trains for teaching and research rather than writing and editing. One-year master's degree programs are likely to be professionally oriented; nearly all doctoral programs are directed toward research and teaching.

Using the Newspaper Fund's *Guide,* write to the graduate schools that you think might be possibilities for you and ask them for their catalogs. Study the courses offered and the other information in these bulletins, and you are virtually certain to find what you want. All that remains is to apply. That should be done during the autumn preceding the year you wish to enroll. In other words, if you are planning to attend in the autumn of 1978, your application should be in before the end of 1977. Most institutions have cutoff dates sometime during the spring, after which it is possible to get in only if someone else drops out or you are able to make an on-the-spot visit and somehow convince the admissions people that you should be accepted—the longest of long shots.

OTHER PREPARATION

What else can you do by way of preparation for a journalism career? Obviously, get any kind of experience you can while you are still in high school. Work on the high school paper and yearbook, any magazine that may exist in your school, or the local newspaper. If you can possibly get a summer job doing anything on a paper in your vicinity, do so. Read a lot, not only general titles, but also books about the newspaper business. The standard newspaper histories listed in the Recommended Reading appendix at the end of this book have good bibliographies, and there is an excellent bibliography called *The Literature of Journalism* (University of Minnesota Press). It may be hard to find, but your local library can get it on an inter-library loan from the state library or the Library of Congress.

Study the medium you're going to work in—the newspaper itself. Read as many of them as you can find, besides the one you read normally. Try to look at them with the beginnings of a professional viewpoint; that is, study the way the stories are written, the manner in which the news is displayed, the general pattern in which it is put together. In short, let the feeling of a newspaper soak into you through a kind of osmosis. If you can't get a part-time or summer newspaper job, at least visit the plant, get to know someone there, see what's happening, and ask questions.

Most people who are serious about going into newspapering won't have to be told to do the things described above. They'll already be doing them. If you feel a reluctance about it, if you're doubtful, take another long look at your interests and career plans. The newspaper business may not be for you.

Finally, be sure you have a good grasp of the tools of the trade. It goes without saying that you must learn to type. Hunt-and-peck is old-fashioned; take a class or get a typing book and learn touch typing. It's easier. Respect the English language and learn how to use it. The most common complaint of newspaper editors about the recruits they get, including those from journalism schools, is that they don't spell well and their grammar is shaky. Writing is a craft, and your responsibility is to master its essential elements—spelling and grammar. Words are going to be the basic tools of your career. It only makes sense to learn to use them properly.

CHAPTER 11

GETTING STARTED

Getting started in the newspaper business is seldom easy. Good times and bad, year in and year out, there always seem to be more talented, eager applicants than there are jobs. Yet there is always competition among employers for the best. Several large newspapers, and especially the chain organizations, send recruiters around to the best schools and departments before graduation to interview prospects.

That this kind of recruiting persists even in times of high unemployment reflects the fact that the communications industry has become so broad, and institutional programs so diverse to match these multiple needs, that the available talent pool splits itself up and not as many are as available to newspapers as in earlier days. Broadcasting claims a large number of graduates now, and so do the nation's 22,000 or so magazines. Others go into advertising, and more are now discovering book publishing as that industry grows ever larger and ever more visible to the public eye.

Newspapers, however, are still the largest employers in communications—larger than most people realize. Nationally, newspapers rank third among the top three employers, after steel and automotive industries.* According to the Newspaper Fund's 1975 employment report, 7 out of 10 news-editorial graduates found media jobs. One went on to graduate school, one found

*U.S. Census Bureau

work elsewhere, and less than one was unemployed. It is expected that, in the future, there will be fewer jobs in the daily field because readership of the dailies continues to drop at a rather alarming rate.

Elsewhere, the outlook is even better. Weeklies and small dailies continue to grow in number and in circulation; *Newsday*, in suburban Long Island, is the fourth largest afternoon daily in the country. The mortality rate among magazines is as high as ever, but the number of new starts far exceeds the losses. That industry can be said to flourish, as periodicals continue to be more and more specialized, reaching more and more small audiences among the immense mass of more than 210 million Americans. Public relations and advertising continue to grow and change, offering a diversity of jobs for graduates. Regular broadcasting is not an expanding business, and it is difficult for newcomers to get into, but cable television offers a new field that, within a few years, should become one of the major sources of employment for communications people.

Viewed against the background of the past, the employment outlook today for those who want to get into journalism is much better, even if it may not seem so to those who are struggling to get their first jobs. However, those journalists who graduated from college in the mid-1930s found themselves in a communications world where television did not yet exist as an employer; where jobs of any kind were scarce because of the Great Depression; and where the number of book publishing, magazine, public relations, and advertising jobs were nowhere equal to what they are today. Yet people found jobs in the media.

Today there are many more jobs available than there were in those days, and while the competition is intense, it is no worse than it was then. The economic conditions of the 1970s, with high unemployment rates, have made things difficult; however, people do get jobs in the media, even though it may not be the kind of job they wanted or in the place where they wanted it.

A part-time or summer job on a newspaper offers valuable experience in preparing for a journalism career.

The field is always overcrowded. At the same time, it is equally true that there is a steady flow of journalism graduates as well as those with different educations into the industry every year. The number of uneducated persons—that is, high school dropouts or less—who "make it" has steadily declined since the beginning of the century. Every business can point to the dropouts who got in and rose to the top through sheer persistence and ability, but their numbers have become fewer and fewer as job requirements have risen.

Traditionally, as earlier chapters have described, people came into the newspaper business at the lowest level, as stringers for wire services or for nearby dailies, as reporters and general handymen on small town weeklies and dailies. The writer of this book managed to do both things simultaneously. This is still the entryway for many people, but as more and more students have had the opportunity to get an education in journalism, and as the media have continued to expand, graduates are less likely to be content with starting at the bottom, and very often, they are not forced to do so.

Most students who go to journalism school want to stay in the metropolitan field, and it is difficult to persuade them to settle for anything else. This is especially true in New York, the media capital of the world, where newspaper opportunities are even scarcer than they were in the past; yet other kinds of communications jobs exist in profusion. The same situation exists in other countries. Spanish graduates of the government's journalism school in Madrid want to stay and work in the capital city, or at least Barcelona; no one wants to go out into the provinces, where there are many more opportunities.

It is easy to understand. There is always the excitement of the city, the enjoyment of its cultural life, the feeling of being in the big time—all that is hard to give up. And today's students are more knowledgeable. When some veteran of the business tells them to go back to the grassroots, start on a small-town paper and work up to the big city, they know that this is too often a prescription for burial. Inland dailies, like the old Kansas City *Star,* were once regarded as training grounds for the big time in New York, but that is no longer true and students know it.

In reality, as far as newspapers are concerned, the big time in New York consists of the *Times,* and *Daily News,* and the *Wall Street Journal*—all unique institutions in their own right.

For those who are intent on metropolitan journalism, the prospects are not inviting and the choices are not numerous. There are a few prestige newspapers in the country to which young reporters can aspire—the *Times* and the *Wall Street Journal* in New York, the *Christian Science Monitor* and possibly the *Globe* in Boston, the Washington *Post,* the Louisville *Courier-Journal,* the Los Angeles *Times,* and three or four others. Needless to say, it is difficult to start on any of these papers, although not impossible by any means. Their staffs are augmented every year by some of the best talent from the best journalism schools.

Where the jobs exist, unfortunately for the metropolitan aspirant, are on the smaller papers across the country that possibly he may never have heard of. Group owners like the Newhouse papers, the Copley papers, the Scripps-Howard organization, the Knight-Ridder group, and the Gannett chain have many more jobs to offer collectively than the top ten metropolitan papers. Then there are hundreds of other papers in the smaller cities and small towns, all of which have to be staffed and whose relatively small salaries and less glamorous, harder work patterns do not attract the graduates in nearly as large numbers.

It comes down to a choice. Either the aspirant tells himself it's going to be a metropolitan daily or nothing and prepares to beat his brains out to get a job on one, or else he decides that it's newspapering for its own sake that he likes, and that he will settle for something else. In such cases, the journalist often treasures in the back of his mind the hope and ambition that, someday, he will get a job on a big paper; often, his ambition is realized.

FINDING A JOB

For the graduate facing these grim prospects who has concluded that no matter what happens he must work on a newspaper of some kind and nowhere else in the media, there are methods he can employ in finding a job. Crass as it may sound, the best approach is to take advantage of any contact he may have with people in the business—a relative, a friend, or a teacher. Nothing is better than a personal introduction and recommendation. Don't hesitate to use any kind of "pull" you can muster. It won't guarantee you a job, but it will get you inside the door for your first interview under the best possible auspices.

If no such entree is available, the shotgun technique offers a tried and proven method used by many graduates. Get a copy of the annual directory of newspapers published by the trade magazine, *Editor & Publisher,* a publication issued in February or

March every year, familiarly known as "the Red Book." You will not be able to buy it on the newsstand, but your library will have it, if it's large enough. If everything else fails, write to the magazine itself, 850 Third Avenue, New York, N.Y., 10022.

The Red Book lists every daily newspaper, divided by states, with addresses, names of the executives, and pertinent information needed by advertisers, for whom it is primarily intended. From the listings, pick out a hundred newspapers in parts of the country where you would like to work, then write a letter of application to the managing editor of each one. The covering letter should state simply your present situation (just graduating, about to graduate, whatever) and what kind of job you're applying for. Don't be afraid to say that you'll take anything available to get a start in the business, if you mean it. Many editors like that attitude. Attach a resume to your letter. The resume should give your name, address, telephone number, age, and marital status. It should carry the details of your education and work experience, emphasizing any media internship you've had. Don't overlook any kind of work, no matter what it may have been, whether relevant to the newspaper business or not. Be sure to list any work you have done on college and high school publications and include your extracurricular activities and any honors you may have achieved. If you have any special talents, like fluency in a foreign language, be sure to put that down too. If you have had anything printed that you think is pretty good, have it copied and send it along, but don't crowd the editor with too much for him to examine.

Having done all this, sit back and wait a little. Out of a hundred letters, experience shows that you may get as many as five or six replies that are encouraging enough to merit a follow-up of one kind or another. This may be in the form of an interview, an invitation to further correspondence, or at the least a promise that you will have first chance at any job openings. Out of these five or six replies, one may result in a job.

On the other hand, you may get only a few replies, none of which may be encouraging. In that case, take another hundred names and repeat the process. Keep at it until your postage money and patience run out. It would be a rare thing if, out of two or three hundred letters, a job did not result.

The only alternative to this method or the personal introduction is to walk in cold at the newspapers nearest you and ask for the personnel director or for the city editor or managing editor. Tell your story, trying to sell yourself. Sometimes it works. At the least, you will probably be asked to fill out a form for personnel, or your application letter or memo will be placed on file. That may seem like a long shot, and it is, but jobs are secured in this fashion every day. It depends on how much of an impression you've made on whoever interviews you, and on the chances of a job opening.

Suppose that your every effort to get a job on a newspaper fails. At that point, some graduates go into their parents' business, switch fields, or go to Vermont to live in a commune. None of these drastic measures is necessary, however. If there are no newspaper jobs available, your aim then should be to find a job in one of the other media, working from that into the newspaper business.

It needs to be said at the outset that the career flow customarily goes the other way. More people go from newspapers into the other media, as we'll be discussing in the next chapter. But if you are determined to have a newspaper career, working in some other medium certainly doesn't preclude it. Magazines are the best place for you in that event, since the work is so similar in many respects. Book publishing is less related, but again, some of the same techniques are used. Broadcasting is quite different, even in the news end, and people do not often go into newspapering from that medium.

If something other than editorial work is your goal, the media are much more interchangeable, but if it is writing and editing you want, the best base to work from is a magazine. Because there are so many more magazines than newspapers, there are also many more jobs, with the added advantage that the high degree of specialization in the business means that you may be able to employ some expertise of your own in your work. For example, a journalism student who described himself as a ski bum failed to get a newspaper job but did get one on a skiing magazine. He was ecstatically happy in this position because he was writing about his major interest and had an opportunity to pursue it and make money at the same time.

People who start on this path to the newspaper business often find that magazine work is more satisfying and, consequently, don't make the continuing effort to get a job on a daily. If the urge to be in the newspaper business persists, however, the jump can be made, especially if the magazine job provides experience which can be useful to a newspaper—editing and copyediting, for example, or writing in a field which the newspaper also covers in its feature departments. Such credits look good on your application as you continue to apply for newspaper jobs, and the experience itself unquestionably makes you more valuable as an employee.

SALARIES

One question remains, What can a new employee expect to earn? It's a most difficult question to answer because the range is so great. At the bottom, on a small daily or weekly, the range is from less than $100 to more than $160 weekly. Even on newspapers which have contracts with the American Newspaper Guild there is no uniformity because scales are adjusted to the size of the paper and local conditions. Guild minimums for beginners may run from $125 a week to $175, and top salaries on newspapers for news executives range from $25,000 a year to $50,000 and up. But even with Guild scales, which have elevated a traditionally low-paying business to a more respectable level, few people on the editorial side of newspapers make what they would in comparable jobs on large magazines, in broadcasting, or in public relations. As in book publishing, that other relatively low-paying segment of the communications industry, newspaper people accept the lower scales because of the nature of the business and the experience of working for a newspaper, which nothing else can duplicate. Otherwise they move on to one of the related fields discussed in the next chapter.

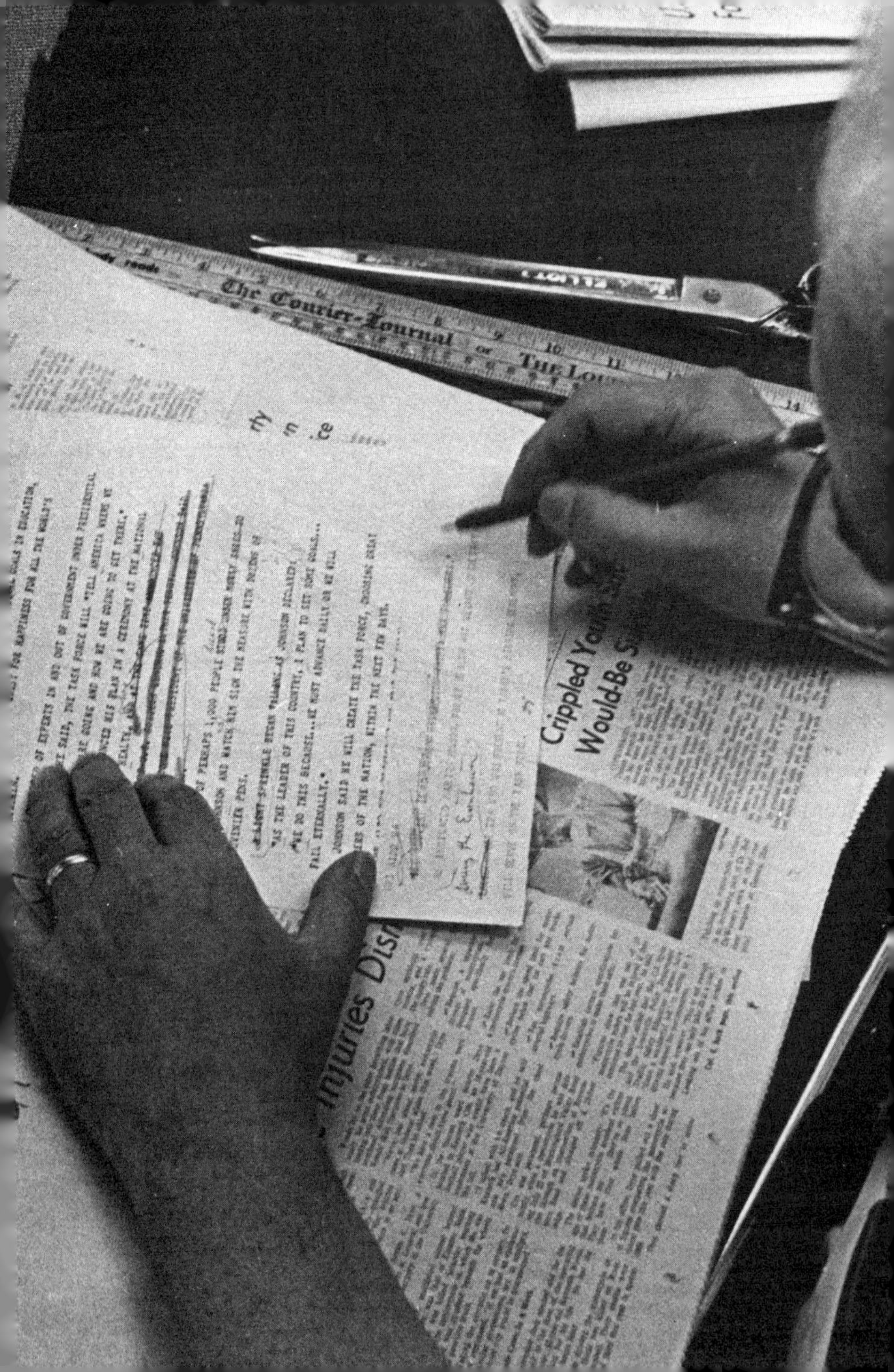
The Courier-Journal

CHAPTER 12

NEWSPAPER WORK AS PREPARATION FOR RELATED FIELDS

The newspaper has always been a training ground for the other media, as well as for writers of books. Many of the best American novelists of this century were newspapermen in their youth, as were a large number of today's writers of popular fiction. Not a few working newspapermen write both fiction and nonfiction as a sideline. In the nonfiction field alone, the number of books produced by newspapermen, former and present, would run into the thousands.

Working for a newspaper prepares people for the other media because it imposes a discipline on writers and editors alike, teaches them to work against time, and gives them a tremendous amount of practice in digging out and organizing facts. Moreover, it brings them close to the human condition and forces them to try to understand and analyze it. After a few years of working on a newspaper, a reporter can say that he has seen how people live at every level, and he will have been exposed to the full range of human character. It is a sobering experience. Newspapermen often are accused by outsiders of being cynical, but it would be more accurate to say that they are realists. They have few illusions.

People leave newspaper work for a variety of reasons, but most often the reason is money. Some dedicated reporters who began at $50 a week during the 1930s let's say, now are approaching retirement from a newspaper and will get some kind of pension, depending on the paper, which will hardly compensate for the $20,000 or $25,000 they are now earning. They were committed to newspaper work from the beginning, and they have stayed with it, through the rise of the Guild, through strikes and contract disputes, through internal power struggles, through all kinds of bosses. Chronic grumblers though they may be, it would be hard to find one who would have chosen another profession.

Meanwhile, many of the reporters they started out with have departed at some point to go into a related field, and many of these people are earning two or three times as much money as their former co-workers who stayed in newspapering. Some own their own public relations businesses or ad agencies. Others are stars of television news; many are big time magazine writers or editors. Money was the primary lure in nearly every case, and to get higher salaries, they were willing to give up the relative job security of a newspaper in favor of the somewhat precarious employment situation in related fields.

But something else is involved, too. The newspaper business, for all its inherent fascination, is not a creative business. The newspaper is an observer and recorder of events, and although it is currently fashionable to talk about "media events," there is very little actual creativity in the content of newspapers. Creative people, bursting with ideas, tend to grow restless in newspaper work, which begins to have a sameness about it after a time. After a few years in a news room, one may have the feeling of seeing the same movie over and over. A foreign correspondent once observed that even wars were alike; they were either larger or smaller, bloodier or dirtier. Robert Garst, a former city editor of the New York *Times,* was once asked by an eager, excited student how the paper had covered the Hindenburg disaster. "Why, it was just a routine job," Mr. Garst observed in his dry manner, thereby bringing down the house and creating a line repeated for years afterward by members of the student's class.

Mr. Garst was telling the simple truth. It *was* a routine job. To the world it was a dramatic catastrophe. To the *Times* men who worked on the story, at least the veterans, it was just another job of getting facts, organizing them, and writing them. The drama was in another medium. Even those alive and present at the time will hardly remember today how the *Times* covered the story (no one will forget the pictures), but it would be difficult to forget the radio announcer's on-the-scene description of the crash, his voice breaking into horrified sobs.

Consequently, both the desire for more money and the need for greater self-expression than newspaper work can provide often impel people to leave this essentially conservative, slow-to-innovate business and move into one of its related fields. Most of them find more money, as well as more trouble; but then, there is almost always a great deal of trouble associated with making money.

There are no reliable statistics to tell us which related field attracts the most newspapermen, but it would be a safe bet that magazines and public relations are numbers one and two, although it would be hard to say which one leads. Let's consider them both as possibilities, beginning with magazines.

MAGAZINES

The magazine business is larger and more varied in job possibilities than any of the other media, and for that reason alone, it is extremely attractive. Among the 22,000 periodicals published, every field of human activity and interest is covered. Consequently, a newspaperman who has built up some expertise in his job can readily find at least one and probably several places where he can transfer for more money and the opportunity to break away from the conventional patterns of news stories.

It is not always understood by people thinking of magazine work that most of it, on the editorial side, does not involve writing. Magazine editors are people who deal in ideas, which is the medium's stock in trade. They think up ideas for their magazines and get writers to write them. They go through the thousands of unsolicited manuscripts sent in to them and find a few that can be developed into articles. They work with writers, agents, and each other to produce a new set of ideas every month or every week, usually against the competition of editors in the same field who are doing the same thing. A hard core of about 300 professional magazine writers supplies the bulk of what is printed, aside from the departments, which are often staff written.

We're speaking here of the 8,000 or so consumer magazines, as they are known in the trade, meaning the familiar titles we all see on the newsstands, directed to audiences within the general public. This, however, is only the tip of the iceberg. The great bulk of magazine production is not seen on the newsstands at all, but is distributed by mail to special audiences in business and industry. At one time, it was called the trade press and had a reputation for low pay and dull work. Today it is known as the business press and is much more highly paid. The work, although specialized, can be absorbing if you are truly interested in the field the magazine covers. A giant of the business press, like McGraw-Hill, publishes more than 40 magazines covering all kinds of business and industrial activity. Its editors and reporters roam the world for news, especially since the advent of multi-national companies, and it maintains its own worldwide press service.

Many newspaper people who gravitate to magazines go to the business press and become specialists in a field that interests them. Fewer go into editing jobs on consumer magazines, since this is a kind of creative job that seems to attract a different kind of person. This is not to say, however, that a good many newspapermen have not become first-class magazine editors. Hundreds of reporters have turned into professional free-lance magazine writers, since this is a natural outgrowth of reporting, and in fact, *is* reporting on another level where there is greater freedom of style than the newspaper allows. The news magazines, too, are well populated with former newspapermen, and again, this is a natural progression. The style is different but the work is essentially the same, and certainly, the salaries are better. News magazine work, however, requires a peculiar kind of temperament to which not all recruits to that business, including newspapermen, can adapt. Making the switch to news magazine work, therefore, involves an element of risk somewhat higher than that of other fields.

Basic writing and editing skills are the same on magazines as they are on newspapers. There is, however, far more variation in both skills on periodicals than the newspaper ever allows, as well as a much greater opportunity for creativity. The two media have many similarities, particularly since television has pushed them closer together. That is the primary reason magazines probably surpass the other media in attracting newspapermen.

TELEVISION AND RADIO

News broadcasting, both television and radio, is full of former newspapermen. Many network news executives started in the newspaper business, and the older generation of television news personalities has a newspaper background. There are fewer among the newer generation because the veterans came into television news at a time when it was new and badly in need of their expertise. Today, since it has become as much show business as it is news, it is quite possible for a young person to gain prominence by rising from the ranks of television itself, without any previous newspaper experience.

Television news is organized in much the same way as a newspaper, and that is why the network news organizations in New York are so full of former New York *Times, Daily News,* and old *Herald Tribune* employees, who may not be on-the-air personalities but who know how to get the news and write it. There are news directors who fulfill the same function as a newspaper's managing editor or city editor; writers who prepare the news that is read on the air from teleprompters or scripts; and reporters who go out on assignments with cameramen. The departure from similarity to newspaper work comes when these reporters face the camera and, half-memorizing or reading, or sometimes ad-libbing, make their verbal reports. In the office, they will also be doing voiceovers for whatever film is used, and they may appear on camera in the studio itself to introduce a film story or comment on it.

The newer generation of television reporters is likely to come directly into the medium without preliminary newspaper experience. Perhaps they have had journalism school courses in television newswriting and production; otherwise they learn on the job. It often is the older people on the news staff who have had the newspaper background, particularly among the older executives, anchormen, and commentators. It is reasonable to suppose that many young reporters will become the executives, anchormen, and commentators of tomorrow, and in time, there will be little, if any, recruiting from newspapers. Television news is, after all, a very young business—hardly more than a quarter-century old—and in its current, high-powered sense, really a product of the 1950s.

Radio always attracts a certain number of journalism graduates who seem to have an affinity for the kind of invisible visibility the medium provides. Newspaper Fund statistics show a slightly larger percentage of graduates go into radio than television. For all but the network radio news organizations and the activities of a relatively few metropolitan stations, radio news consists of five minutes of reading from the AP or UPI wire, usually by an announcer who has trouble with the foreign names. Most stations (except the small independents) are affiliated with the networks, however, and they receive and broadcast the newscasts that emanate from New York and Washington. In some cases, networks use the voices of their television reporters on the radio. Since everything that goes on the air is read, no matter who reads it, radio stations and networks must employ staffs of writers and editors. It is to these jobs that newspaper people are most apt to gravitate. The work is so much the same, except for the easily acquired special technique which goes into writing for a time space and the human voice, rather than for the printed page.

PUBLIC RELATIONS AND ADVERTISING

Public relations (PR) and advertising, especially the former, attract more newspaper people than any medium except the magazines.

Each year, public relations absorbs more and more graduates of journalism schools and departments. Once again the reason is money, although the reports of what beginners and lower echelon people are paid in PR often are highly exaggerated. Nevertheless, overall there is more money to be made in public relations than in working for newspapers, and there is also a great deal more variety.

Today, the field of public relations covers a wide area of human activity. There is the field of corporate public relations, extending from the largest corporate giants to the smallest companies. Multi-national business organizations have made this an international occupation, and the biggest companies have large public relations staffs. Then there are the public relations agencies, which service corporate and other clients, either handling their entire program or supplementing what their PR staff does. Major advertising agencies also have PR divisions which help with the problems of clients. Institutions of every kind, from universities to trade organizations, employ PR people, including government at every level, where the phrase "public relations" may not always be used, but the work is the same.

However that may be, newspaper work is excellent preparation for public relations in several ways. Although writing press releases is far from being the major activity of PR people, as outsiders often think it is, releases *are* written in immense quantities. Since they are essentially news stories about products, people, or policies, those with newspaper training usually are able to write them easily. When it is necessary to sell a story to a paper, or to talk to a city editor or some other executive about something involving a client, ex-newspaper people often have the necessary contacts and know how to talk to the person at the other end.

Much of public relations consists of presenting a corporation, an individual, or an institution to the public in the best possible light. In this activity, a PR person with newspaper experience can be helpful because he has the perspective to be able to tell his client how the public is likely to view a certain policy or action. As a reporter, he has dealt with both the public, in its broadest aspects, and with upper level people in business and government; consequently, he often is able to devise programs and policies which will make his client's path smoother. The former newspaperman, if he is a good writer, also can be helpful in writing speeches and in supervising the production of all kinds of printed matter flowing from a PR operation. Moreover, his experience with people will help him to arrange smoothly functioning press conferences, product introductions, and in fact, any kind of contact between client and public. All these are the essence of public relations work.

Most people who shift from newspapers to PR go into corporate or agency work. The former can be highly lucrative. Vice-presidents in charge of public relations, the ultimate goal, can earn as much as $100,000 a year and up, and even those on subordinate levels are very well paid by newspaper standards.

Those who go into agency work generally follow one of two well defined paths. They become account executives, and if things go well, eventually officers of the agency; otherwise, they leave to start their own firms, taking one or two lucrative clients with them. As individual entrepreneurs, the sky is the limit, depending on their own skill and energy, as well as a certain amount of luck. It is also quite possible to lose everything and find yourself back in somebody else's agency. In any case, there are opportunities for fame and fortune which simply don't exist on newspapers.

As in broadcasting, graduating students today tend to go directly into PR work without newspaper training, and they can do very well without it. On the other hand, for those who find the newspaper confining after a time, public relations offers another, related field into which it is not too difficult to translate yourself.

While some newspapermen come into the advertising field at the copywriting end and do well, there is little about newspaper work that prepares anyone for the advertising business. Except for copywriting, advertising is essentially a salesman's game, and that is not particularly a characteristic field for newspaper people.

Again, it ought to be emphasized: Newspaper work will prepare you for related fields in the ways described here. But those who have doubts about whether they want to be in newspaper work are probably not right for the business. If they have other inclinations, they should decide exactly what it is they want to do and go into it directly.

CHAPTER 13

THE FUTURE OF NEWSPAPERS
—HOW TO PREPARE FOR IT

Tom Wicker, the New York *Times* columnist, writing from the Republican Convention of 1976, reported that "not a few reporters here are filing their stories by punching a computer." Nothing could have dramatized as well the rapid progress of technology in the newspaper business.

Today, more and more newspapers are introducing computers into their newswriting and typesetting operations. Only the resistance of the mechanical unions and the high cost of the equipment have prevented automated typesetting from completely sweeping the industry. The unions are now beginning to bow to the inevitable, and some of the major metropolitan dailies are well advanced toward automating their composing rooms. Smaller papers, using offset equipment, have also come a long way down this path. High equipment costs are still a barrier to most papers, but inevitably, one supposes, the prices will come down.

Now the technological march is advancing on the newsroom, and the newspapers able to afford it are already using advanced equipment, as Wicker indicated. The reporter typing out his story on a computer punchboard in Kansas City knows that his words are going to be transmitted directly to a machine in his home office which will decode the tape and cause the stories to emerge on an editing screen. There they will be edited with an electronic pencil, after which they will go by tape to an automatic typesetting machine.

Other inventions are in the offing. One hears of reporters calling in stories to machines which translate the voice into typed words which can then be rearranged and edited by computer. Electronics are beginning to transform a business which has changed more slowly than almost any other, and it will never be the same again.

All this has put the journalism schools and departments in something of a dilemma. The new electronic gadgets are expensive, and with the kind of limited budgets educational institutions operate on these days, very few journalism schools can afford to buy, install, and maintain such equipment to train their students. At the moment it is not a crisis because few students will be going to work for newspapers where the equipment is available. When it arrives, they will be able to learn on the job, as staff members everywhere will have to do. But eventually, as the technology becomes more widespread, the schools will either have to buy the equipment and train students, or else newspapers will have to institute special training programs.

In any case, it is just possible that the new electronic systems have arrived too late, and that the newspaper as we have always known it is an anachronism that will be replaced in the next quarter-century.

Various scenarios have been drawn up for this transformation. They all begin with agreement that the whole business of getting a newspaper into print and transporting it from a plant by truck, newsstand, delivery boy, and whatever other means may be necessary is cumbersome and old-fashioned and becoming pro-hibitively expensive as well. It is especially difficult in countries where great distances or the lack of adequate transportation make rapid distribution difficult.

Some countries have tried to solve these problems by means of facsimile transmission, in which the image of a newspaper page is transmitted by wire to some distant point where it is reproduced immediately for publication. By using this method, Moscow newspapers are able to publish simultaneously in that city and those far away in the U.S.S.R.'s Eastern provinces; Norwegian papers can do the same with their northern cities separated from the south by mountain ranges; and Tokyo papers are published simultaneously in such remote places as the northern island of Honshu.

In America, both the *Wall Street Journal* and the *Christian Science Monitor* use facsimile transmission to cover the country, thus making themselves truly national newspapers. But while this kind of newspaper delivery is successful, it only makes it possible to publish in the normal way in several distant cities simultaneously. The next technological step is to bypass such transmission entirely and bring the newspaper directly from the newspaper office into the home.

The technology already exists to make this possible, with some essential refinements still to come. Cable television, which is on the rise, has for the first time made such newspaper-to-home transmission feasible. Basically, it would require every home user to have a television set and a slave machine, which would give the TV viewer, at the touch of a button, a printout of any newspaper page appearing on the screen.

The process would work in this way. Newspaper pages would be prepared in the usual manner in newspaper offices and would be constantly available on a twenty-four-hour basis to cable customers, who would merely tune in to a certain channel to get their paper. On the screen before them would appear the front page, let's say, and it would remain fixed on the screen until the user employed his remote control device to let it roll on. Re-made front pages would appear every hour or so, whenever the flow of news justified it. This could also be done by direct transmission from satellites, as well as by cable.

Subsequent transmission of pages would be by category. That is, the sports pages would be shown, then food and fashion, then editorials, and so on. Advertising would appear on pages by itself. Equipped with his remote control device, the home reader could let these pages slip by on the screen as rapidly or as slowly as he desired. If he wanted to save a page for later study—this would be particularly true of advertisements, for example, or possibly reviews of the arts or of restaurants—he would simply press the button on his slave machine, and a copy of the page would be made and fed out to him, computer style.

The advantages to both reader and newspaper are obvious. For the reader, he would never have to wait for the paper but would always have it on tap, with its pages brought up-to-date regularly, and the possibility of taking away with him any part of it he desired. For the newspaper, it would mean removing at least part of the advantage television possesses, that is, timeliness in reporting the news. There is no way, of course, by which the chief advantage, live broadcasting of news events, could be overcome. But more than that, the financial savings to newspapers would be enormous. Composing room, mailing room, and the present circulation system would no longer be needed.

That is only one of several projections communications experts have made in forecasting the future of newspapers. Whichever scenario one chooses to accept, however, the conclusion is that in the future, by one technology or another, newspapers are going to be transmitted directly into the home from newspaper offices and be available around the clock. Most experts are convinced that it is no longer a question of whether this is going to happen, but only when.

There remain a few skeptics. So many technological improvements in communications have been advertised as just around the corner, and as yet are not in view, that there is room to be wary of more promises. After all, there were no significant technological changes in printing from the time Gutenberg invented his press in the fifteenth century until 1825, and no radical departures from that date until recent times. But one should never forget that we live in an age of breathless technological advance, and progress (or change, if you will) has been telescoped as never before in human history. We even have a popular phrase for it, "future shock." So it is reasonable to assume that the new day in newspaper publishing is going to arrive, although it may not be as imminent as enthusiasts think it is. Substantial difficulties lie in the way. Cable systems have to be much more common than they are now, and the price of home equipment will have to be reasonable. As it was in television, someone will have to assume the expense until mass production is possible. A way will have to be found, too, for the reader to pay for his electronic newspaper, but pay television already suggests the answer.

What does all this mean for the student contemplating a newspaper career today? For one thing, it means that he will be working with instruments that are going to make the ordinary typewriter obsolete, and he will have to learn how to use them one way or the other. He should now be reading the trade magazines, like *Editor & Publisher,* to keep up with progress in advancing technology, so that he at least knows what is being done. Students going into newspapering today are like no other generation that has preceded them. They are in the vanguard of a technological explosion that is going to revolutionize the business.

In a world of change, however, there are some constants. For instance, no one has suggested that there is any mechanical substitute for a reporter. Not even the most formidable computer is capable of what the human brain is able to do, and although some scientists might dispute it, there is not much likelihood there ever will be. A reporter covering a story goes out to cover an event, talks to people, reflects on what he has seen and heard, organizes the facts in his mind, and writes his story. This is what cannot be done by machines. Physical movement is, of course, impossible for machines, but what separates man from the other animals is his ability to reflect, and that is what a reporter does, among other things, when he puts a story together.

Computers have written stories of a sort after words and ideas have been programmed into them, and while that is a mechanical marvel, it doesn't approach what any reporter does when he sits down to write a story. Unquestionably, new technology is going to take over after that point. Stories will be written on computer-tied terminals and other new machines, they will be edited electronically and set automatically. But the preliminary process, by far the most important part, is a human one and will remain so.

With that in mind, it seems more than ever, in the new society which he is entering, the young newspaperman should be doubly concerned about *what* he writes. We have developed, and are continuing to develop, the most fantastic communications system the world has ever known. We are already capable of prodigies of transmission. People talk a great deal about the *means* of communication, about the *process* of it, but not much is heard about the quality of what is being communicated. What good will it do us to have electronic marvels if what we transmit is inadequate, or even nonsense?

The task of newspapers is to inform the people what is going on in the world and to explain it, as far as that is possible, so that people can make intelligent decisions about their lives. That may sound hopelessly idealistic, but if newspapers are not that, they are merely transmission belts for trivia, entertainment, and ego trips. If you believe that information and explanation are the true reason for the existence of newspapers, it places a tremendous responsibility on you who are going to work for them. To inform and explain about a world as incredibly complex as the one we live in, and to do it accurately and clearly, calls for dedication, hard work, and an unremitting adherence to the highest personal standards of craftsmanship. It is this kind of person that newspapers need more than anything else today—more than new gadgets, new machines, new transmission systems, or anything else. To be one of those people is as worthy a cause as a young man or woman can dedicate himself to in our time.

APPENDIX A

RECOMMENDED READING

HISTORY OF JOURNALISM

Emery, Edwin. *The Press and America,* 3rd ed. Englewood Cliffs, N.J.: Prentice-Hall, 1972.

Mott, Frank L. *American Journalism,* rev. ed. New York: Macmillan, 1967.

Tebbel, John. *A Compact History of the American Newspaper.* New York: Hawthorn, 1963.

____. *The Media in America.* New York: T. Y. Crowell, 1974.

CAREER INFORMATION

A Newspaper Career and You. The Newspaper Fund (P.O. Box 300, Princeton, N.J. 08540).

A Reporter Reports. American Council on Education for Journalism (School of Journalism, University of Missouri, Columbia, Mo. 65201).

Brucker, Herbert. *Journalist.* New York: Macmillan, 1962.

Careers for Negroes on Newspapers. The Newspaper Guild (1126 - 16th St. N.W., Washington, D.C. 20036).

Careers in Journalism—Newspapers. Quill and Scroll Society (University of Iowa, Iowa City, Iowa 52242).

Gemill, H., and B. Kilgore, eds. *Do You Belong in Journalism?* New York: Appleton-Century-Crofts.

Grumich, C. A., ed. *Reporting/Writing from Front Row Seats.* New York: Simon and Schuster.

Hulteng, H. W., and R. P. Nelson. *The Fourth Estate: An Informal Appraisal of the News and Opinion Media.* New York: Harper and Row, 1971.

Stein, M. L. *Your Career in Journalism.* New York: Messner, 1965.

Tebbel, John. *Opportunities in Publishing Careers.* Louisville: Vocational Guidance Manuals, 1975.

There is a Career Waiting for You with America's Community Press. National Newspaper Association (491 National Press Building, Washington, D.C. 20004).

Your Future in Daily Newspapers. American Newspaper Publishers Association Foundation (P.O. Box 17407, Dulles Airport, Washington, D.C. 20041).

1976 Journalism Scholarship Guide and Directory of College Journalism Programs. The Newspaper Fund (P.O. Box 300, Princeton, N.J. 08540).

INDEX